AWESOME
SPACE
TECH

AWESOME SPACE TECH

 **40**

AMAZING

INFOGRAPHICS

FOR KIDS

Jenn Dlugos and Charlie Hatton

PRUFROCK PRESS INC.
WACO, TEXAS

Library of Congress Cataloging-in-Publication Data

Names: Dlugos, Jenn, author. | Hatton, Charlie, author.
Title: Awesome space tech : 40 amazing infographics for kids / Jenn Dlugos
  and Charlie Hatton.
Description: Waco, TX : Prufrock Press Inc., [2019] | Includes
  bibliographical references. | Audience: Age 9-12.
Identifiers: LCCN 2018058058 (print) | LCCN 2019005521 (ebook) | ISBN
  9781618218766 (eBook) | ISBN 9781618218759 (print)
Subjects: LCSH: Outer space--Juvenile literature. | Outer space--Pictorial
  works--Juvenile literature.
Classification: LCC QB500.22 (ebook) | LCC QB500.22 .D58 2019 (print) | DDC
  520--dc23
LC record available at https://lccn.loc.gov/2018058058

Edited by Stephanie McCauley

Cover, layout design, and illustrations by Micah Benson

ISBN-13: 978-1-61821-875-9

Printed in the United States of America.

At the time of this book's publication, all facts and figures cited are the most current available. All telephone numbers, addresses, and website URLs are accurate and active. All publications, organizations, websites, and other resources exist as described in the book, and all have been verified. The authors and Prufrock Press Inc. make no warranty or guarantee concerning the information and materials given out by organizations or content found at websites, and we are not responsible for any changes that occur after this book's publication. If you find an error, please contact Prufrock Press Inc.

Source of Production: 1010 Printing Asia Limited, North Point, Hong Kong, China
Date of Production: May 2019
Run Number: 5014852

Printed and bound in China

Prufrock Press Inc.
P.O. Box 8813
Waco, TX 76714-8813
Phone: (800) 998-2208
Fax: (800) 240-0333
http://www.prufrock.com

TABLE OF CONTENTS

INTRODUCTION

Rings around Saturn. Texts on your cell phone. Planets orbiting a faraway star. A car's navigation system. Galaxies spinning in the void. What do these things have in common? (Besides being the answers to the nerdiest *Jeopardy!* category ever, that is.)

The common thread tying all of these things together is space technology. Without our abilities to peer deep into space, to launch spacecraft into orbit and beyond, and to occasionally leave the comfort of Earth's atmosphere ourselves, nothing on the list above would exist in our lives. (Of course, planets and stars and galaxies would still exist, somewhere out there. But without space tech, we'd know almost nothing about them. Pretty twinkling lights are all we'd see.)

Luckily, humans have managed to develop quite a lot of space-based technology. The science behind telescopes is advancing all of the time, allowing us to look closer and see deeper into the wonders of space than ever before. Satellites of all shapes, sizes, and functions whiz around Earth's atmosphere. Probes, rovers, space telescopes, and other craft explore the mysteries of our solar system and beyond. And manned missions, including those to the International Space Station, allow a lucky few to escape Earth's atmosphere for a while and learn firsthand what living in space is like.

Of course, the technology used to cast our views, our craft, and ourselves into space is constantly changing. From the first small telescopes 400 years ago, to the first shaky space launches in the 1950s, to today's house-sized observatories and remote-controlled rovers scouring another world, space tech has evolved quickly and led to countless amazing discoveries.

In this book, we'll explore the world of space technology—how it works, what it's used for, what's new (and what's old), what's next, and how it's changed the way we live. You might only see stars or blue sky when you look up, but there's a lot more happening up there— and space tech (and the people behind it) is responsible. Let's have a look!

Hi, I'm Aster! Let's race! —last one in space is a Sputnik-head!

1 FUELS RUSH IN

It's a long way up to space. Whether you're putting a satellite in orbit, launching a probe, or visiting a space station, you need a rocket to get off the Earth and up there. And in that rocket, you'll need an awful lot of fuel. Here's what most rockets use to give them oomph.

So, how many parsecs per gallon does this thing get?

Solid-Fuel Rocket

Solid-fuel rockets usually use powdered aluminum as the fuel. An oxidizer (a substance that reacts with the aluminum, making it burn to create energy) is mixed with the fuel and packed into the rocket. Add a spark to light the fuel, and blast off!

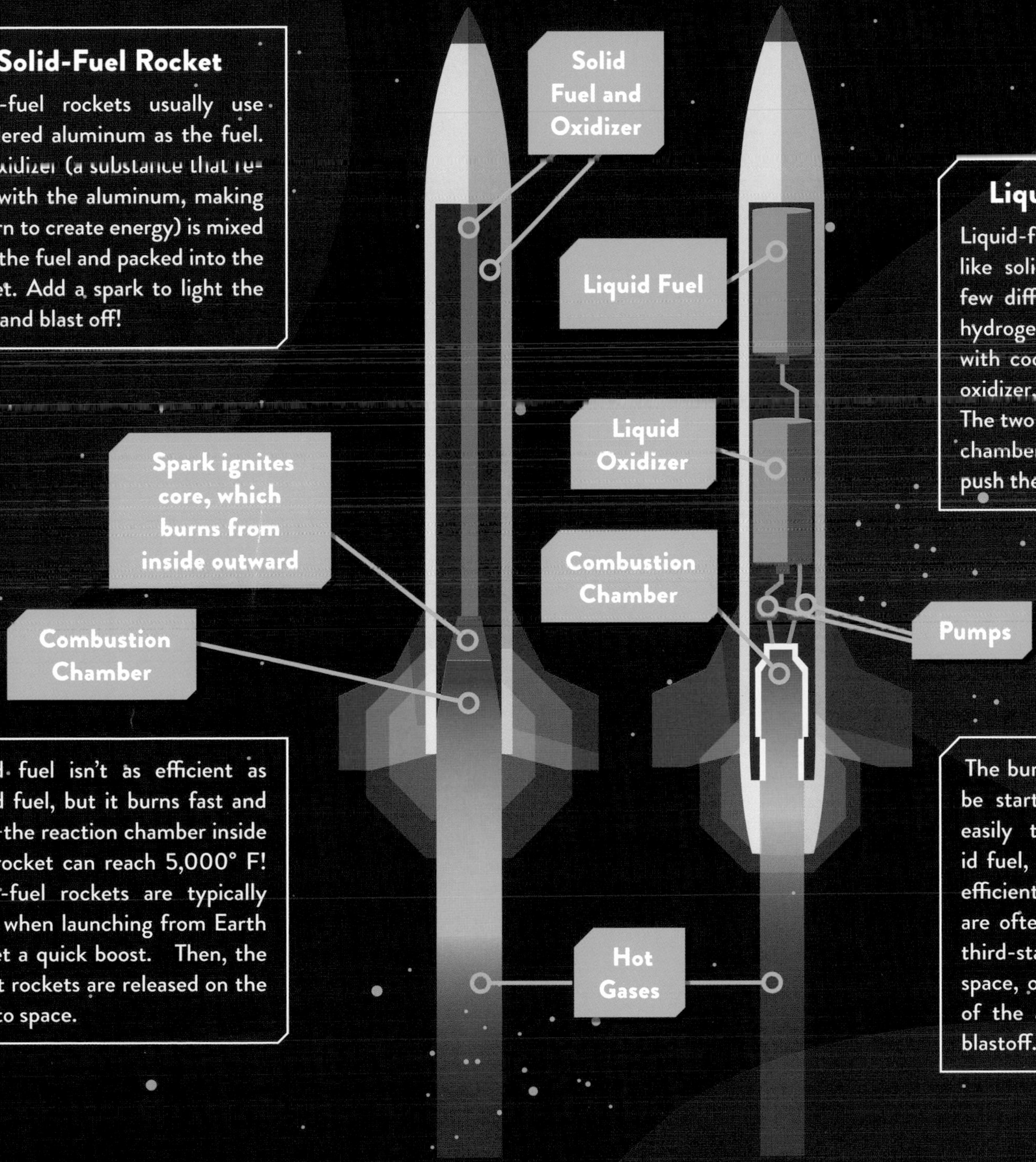

Solid fuel isn't as efficient as liquid fuel, but it burns fast and hot—the reaction chamber inside the rocket can reach 5,000° F! Solid-fuel rockets are typically used when launching from Earth to get a quick boost. Then, the spent rockets are released on the way to space.

Liquid-Fuel Rocket

Liquid-fuel rockets work much like solid-fuel rockets, with a few differences. Cooled liquid hydrogen is typically the fuel, with cooled liquid oxygen, the oxidizer, in a separate tank. The two are mixed in a separate chamber to produce energy and push the rocket forward.

The burns from liquid fuel can be started and stopped more easily than those from solid fuel, and liquid fuel is more efficient. Liquid-fuel boosters are often used in second- and third-stage rockets that fire in space, or in the upper reaches of the atmosphere, well after blastoff.

Solid Fuel and Oxidizer

Liquid Fuel

Spark ignites core, which burns from inside outward

Liquid Oxidizer

Combustion Chamber

Combustion Chamber

Pumps

Hot Gases

3

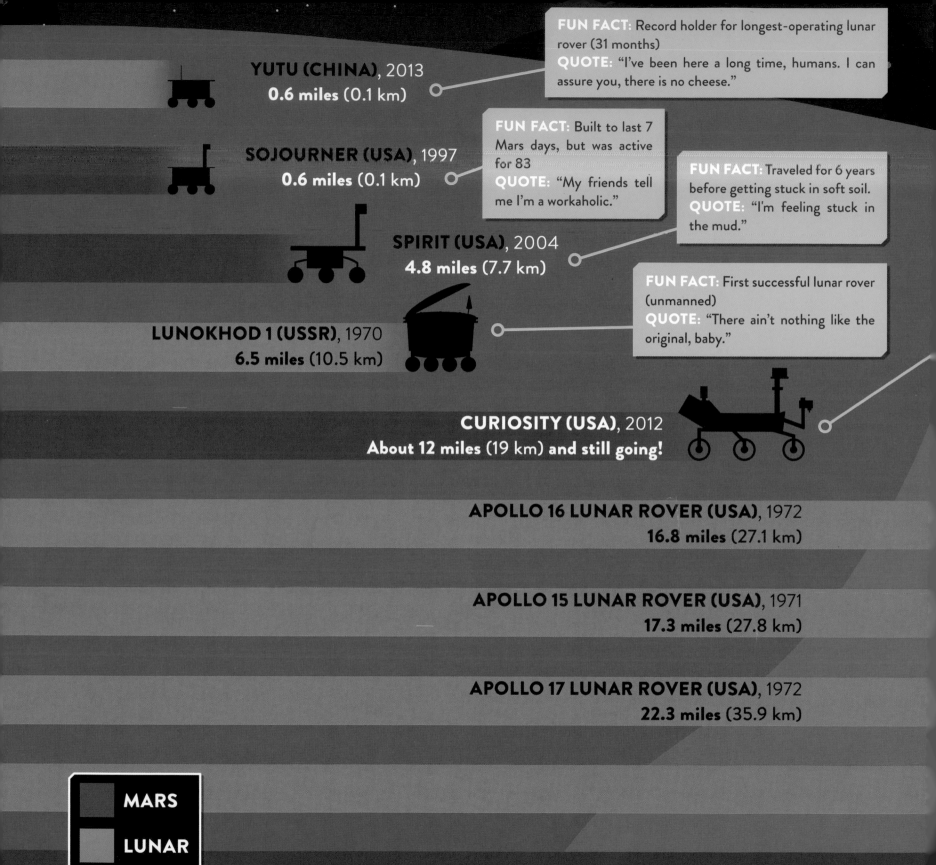

YUTU (CHINA), 2013
0.6 miles (0.1 km)

FUN FACT: Record holder for longest-operating lunar rover (31 months)
QUOTE: "I've been here a long time, humans. I can assure you, there is no cheese."

SOJOURNER (USA), 1997
0.6 miles (0.1 km)

FUN FACT: Built to last 7 Mars days, but was active for 83
QUOTE: "My friends tell me I'm a workaholic."

FUN FACT: Traveled for 6 years before getting stuck in soft soil.
QUOTE: "I'm feeling stuck in the mud."

SPIRIT (USA), 2004
4.8 miles (7.7 km)

FUN FACT: First successful lunar rover (unmanned)
QUOTE: "There ain't nothing like the original, baby."

LUNOKHOD 1 (USSR), 1970
6.5 miles (10.5 km)

CURIOSITY (USA), 2012
About 12 miles (19 km) and still going!

APOLLO 16 LUNAR ROVER (USA), 1972
16.8 miles (27.1 km)

APOLLO 15 LUNAR ROVER (USA), 1971
17.3 miles (27.8 km)

APOLLO 17 LUNAR ROVER (USA), 1972
22.3 miles (35.9 km)

MARS
LUNAR

2 THE COOLEST ROAD TRIPS EVER

When you need to cruise along the surface of the moon or Mars, you need a cool set of wheels. Here are the distances traveled by the space rovers so far.

FUN FACT: Primary mission is to determine if Mars can (or once did) support life
QUOTE: "Perfect for the extraterrestrial biologist on the go!"

FUN FACT: First rover to explore the highlands areas of the moon
QUOTE: "I carried 200 pounds of moon rocks—plenty of room for souvenirs!"

FUN FACT: First manned lunar rover
QUOTE: "I'm the original party bus!"

FUN FACT: Record holder for the farthest traveled space rover
QUOTE: "None of these rovers can catch me!"

FUN FACT: Achieved fastest lunar land speed (11 mph or 17.7 km/h)
QUOTE: "Just call me Lightning MoonQueen"

FUN FACT: Record holder for longest rover trip on the moon
QUOTE: "Wanna go far? Hop in this space car."

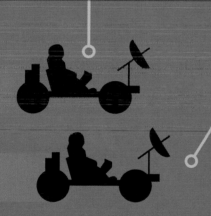

LUNOKHOD 2 (USSR), 1973
26 miles (42 km)

OPPORTUNITY (USA), 2004
More than 28 miles (45 km)

5

FASTER THAN A SPACEFARING BULLET

Measuring speed on Earth is easy enough—but in space, speed depends on your point of reference. Are you traveling relative to Earth? Relative to the sun? Relative to the center of the galaxy? Whatever your reference point, the spacecraft here are (or soon will be) seriously fast.

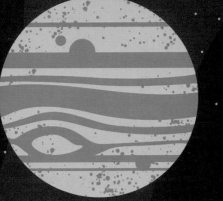

Voyager 1

Holding the record for speeding directly away from the sun is our farthest-out spacecraft, Voyager 1. Launched in 1977, Voyager 1 is moving away at more than 38,000 mph.

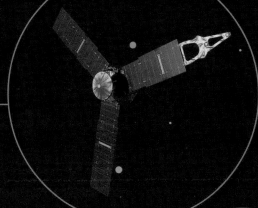

Juno

Gravity's pull can speed up any nearby object, and in 2016, the Juno spacecraft raced to about 165,000 mph, relative to Earth, as gas giant Jupiter's gravity pulled it closer. Soon after, Juno slowed into a stable orbit.

New Horizons

The record holder for fastest launch speed is NASA's New Horizons mission, which zoomed away from Earth in 2006 at around 36,000 mph (and away from the sun at nearly 100,000 mph).

Stardust

What goes up fast comes down fast, too. In 2006, the Stardust craft's sample return capsule, full of material collected from comet Wild 2, reentered Earth's atmosphere at a record speed (for manmade objects) of almost 29,000 mph.

Parker Solar Probe

In 2018, NASA launched the Parker Solar Probe, which will fly close enough to the sun to touch its atmosphere—and reach orbital speeds up to 450,000 mph!

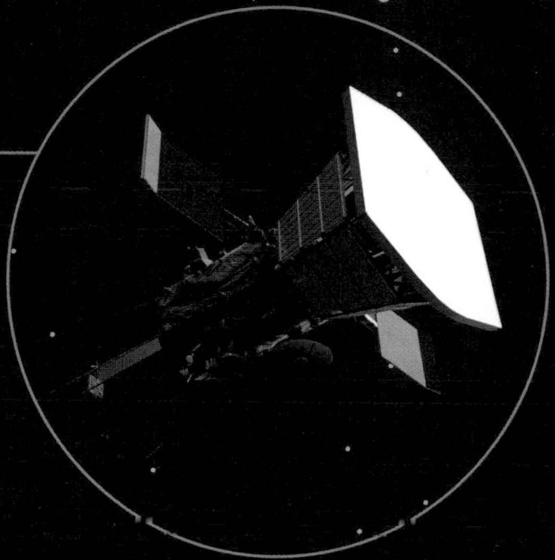

Helios 1 and Helios 2

If gravity equals speed, there's no better destination than the sun (or as close as possible). Launched in the 1970s, NASA's Helios 1 and Helios 2 probes orbited the sun at 157,000 mph (relative to the sun).

I could run that fast . . . if I were wearing my good sneakers.

The fastest unmanned jet on Earth (the X-43A) only flew over 7,000 mph. Score one for spacecraft!

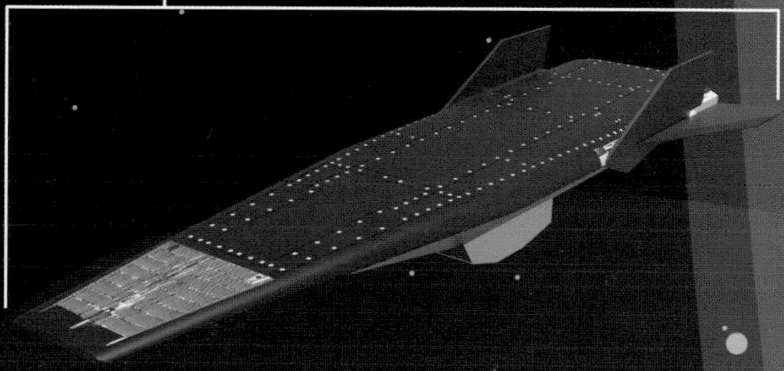

SOLID GOLD RECORD

When the Voyager program launched in 1977, NASA included a golden record inside of each craft that contains images, music, sounds, and audio greetings from Earth. On the cover of each record, there are visual instructions to help curious aliens figure out how to play it.

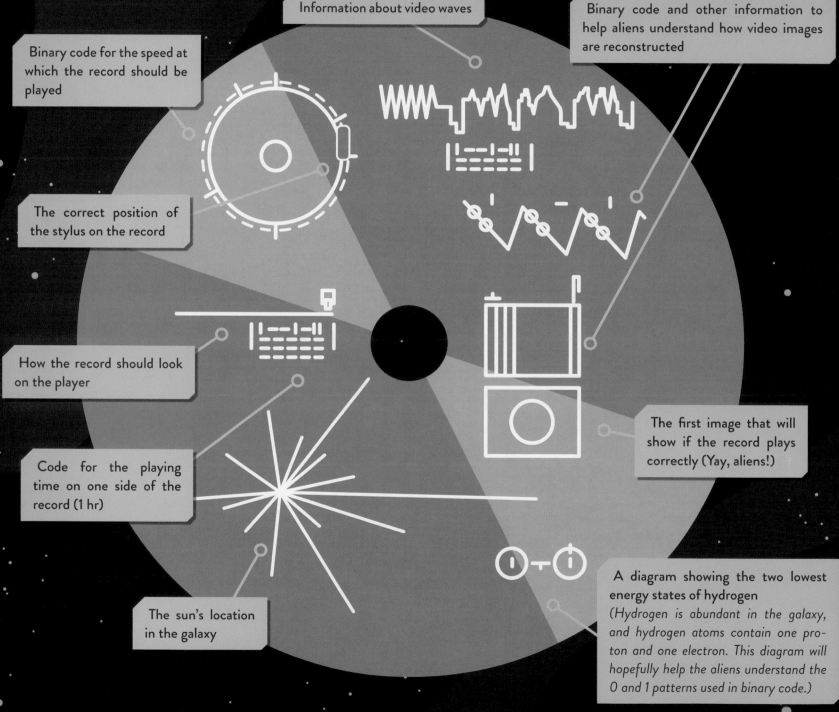

Information about video waves

Binary code and other information to help aliens understand how video images are reconstructed

Binary code for the speed at which the record should be played

The correct position of the stylus on the record

How the record should look on the player

Code for the playing time on one side of the record (1 hr)

The sun's location in the galaxy

The first image that will show if the record plays correctly (Yay, aliens!)

A diagram showing the two lowest energy states of hydrogen (Hydrogen is abundant in the galaxy, and hydrogen atoms contain one proton and one electron. This diagram will hopefully help the aliens understand the 0 and 1 patterns used in binary code.)

5 TO FIND WALDO, JUST CHECK YOUR WATCH

You may have heard of the Global Positioning System (or GPS)—a network of satellites used to locate cars, planes, cell phones, and most anything else near the surface of the Earth. But did you know that the key to GPS is a set of incredibly accurate clocks zinging by overhead?

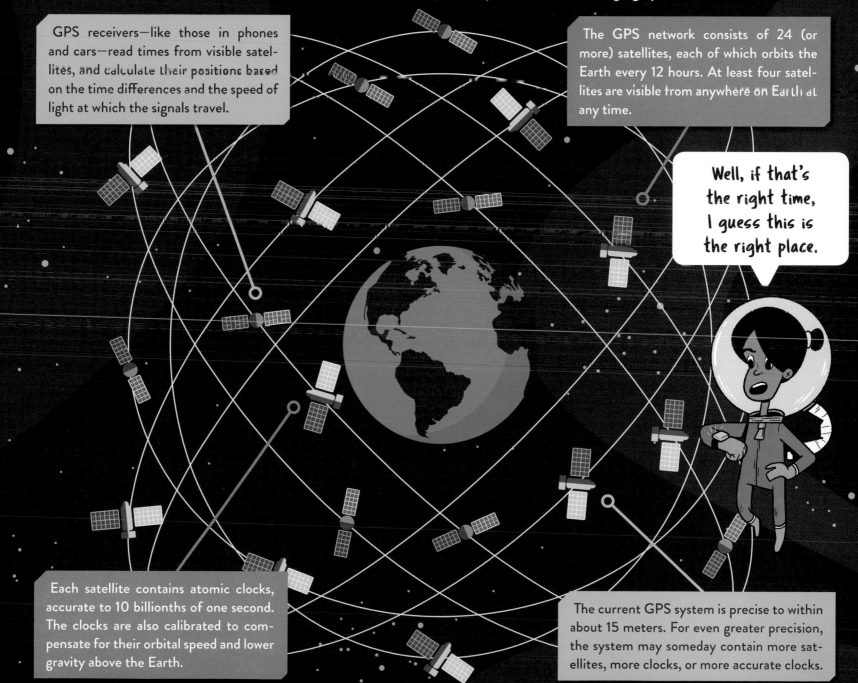

GPS receivers—like those in phones and cars—read times from visible satellites, and calculate their positions based on the time differences and the speed of light at which the signals travel.

The GPS network consists of 24 (or more) satellites, each of which orbits the Earth every 12 hours. At least four satellites are visible from anywhere on Earth at any time.

Well, if that's the right time, I guess this is the right place.

Each satellite contains atomic clocks, accurate to 10 billionths of one second. The clocks are also calibrated to compensate for their orbital speed and lower gravity above the Earth.

The current GPS system is precise to within about 15 meters. For even greater precision, the system may someday contain more satellites, more clocks, or more accurate clocks.

WEIRD AND WONDERFUL USES FOR GPS

Understanding the Air Up There

When a GPS satellite sends a radio signal to Earth, molecules in the atmosphere alter the signal. Scientists study these alterations to learn more about the composition of our atmosphere.

Tracking Bird Migration

Scientists can put tiny GPS transmitters on birds to track their migration. This can help scientists understand more about how birds survive, reproduce, and communicate. They can also analyze how climate and other environmental changes affect bird migration patterns over time.

Predicting Volcanic Eruptions

GPS can detect deformations in the ground caused by magma moving underneath the Earth's surface. Scientists use this information to predict whether a volcanic eruption is imminent.

Can GPS help me find my space socks?

Find Your Ball

It's no fun looking for your golf ball in the rough, so companies are now making golf balls with GPS chips to help golfers find their lost balls quickly.

Preventing Shark Attacks

Many large sharks are tagged with GPS monitors that track their locations. These monitors can help scientists determine whether a shoreline has an elevated risk of a shark attack.

Measuring Hurricane Wind Speeds

Hurricane winds distort GPS signals. Scientists analyze these distortions to determine the wind speed of the hurricane.

Geocaching

Geocaching is a worldwide treasure hunt. A participant will hide a small treasure box in a location. He or she will then post the GPS coordinates for the box on a website so that other geocachers can find it.

7 ALL THE WORLD'S A STAGE (BUT SPACE NEEDS TWO OR THREE)

Many rockets have just one "stage," or an engine with a fuel source. But all rockets to date launched from Earth into space have been multistage rockets. Getting into orbit—or beyond—needs that extra "oomph!" that multiple stages provide.

The advantage of multiple stages is that when fuel is used in one stage, it can be released, lowering the remaining weight. In serial-stage rockets, one stage fires, is jettisoned, and the next stage kicks in.

In parallel-stage rockets, like those used to deliver NASA's space shuttles into space, "booster" rockets fire along with the main stage, then drop away when their fuel is spent.

Some rockets use both serial and parallel stages, or clusters of several rockets as a first stage, to improve efficiency further and to deliver larger payloads into space.

With recent improvements in engine technology, scientists are developing the first "single stage to orbit" (SSTO) rocket, without need for multiple stages.

And the first stage, connected to the second stage . . .

THE RACE TO SPACE, ALL OVER THE PLACE

The original "space race" of the 1950s and 1960s saw the United States and Soviet Union one-upping each other to reach and explore space. The Soviets were first to launch a satellite into orbit in 1957, but the U.S. won the race to land humans on the moon just 12 years later. Today, several nations are space-capable.

European Space Agency (ESA)

Formed: 1975

- Launched orbiter Cassini (with NASA, 2004) to orbit Saturn and landed Huygens probe on Saturn's moon Titan (2005)
- Launched Rosetta mission to orbit a comet (2004–2016)
- International Space Station partner

National Aeronautics and Space Administration (NASA)

Formed: 1958

- Successfully landed astronauts on the moon (Apollo missions, 1969–1972)
- Launched and maintained space lab Skylab (1973–1979)
- Operated space shuttles (1981–2011)
- International Space Station partner

Hold on a minute—where's Starfleet Command?

China National Space Administration (CNSA)

Formed: 1993
- Launched and maintained space labs Tiangong-1 (2011–2016) and Tiangong-2 (2016–present)
- Successfully soft-landed rover Yutu on the moon (2014)

Japanese Aerospace Exploration Agency (JAXA)

Formed: 2003
- Launched satellites to study Earth, our atmosphere, and space
- Sent astronauts on multiple NASA space shuttle missions
- International Space Station partner

Roscosmos

Formed: 1992 (known as the Soviet space program from 1931–1991)
- Launched first successful satellite (Sputnik 1, 1957), first human into space (1961), first space station (Salyut 1, 1971), and Mir space station (1986–2001)
- International Space Station partner

A HOME AWAY FROM HOME

Space stations give astronauts a view of Earth's surface from afar and allow them to see a much clearer picture of space objects than we can see here on the ground. Here are some of the space stations used throughout history.

Skylab 1

COUNTRY: USA
YEAR OF LAUNCH: 1973
FUN FACT: First U.S. space station
HISTORY: A meteoroid shield on Skylab accidentally opened during launch, causing the shield to rip off. This could have been catastrophic for the space station, but the first crew successfully repaired it, and Skylab stayed in orbit for 6 years. Skylab fell out of orbit prematurely in 1979 due to intense solar activity. NASA tried to adjust the station to fall in an unpopulated area, but a math mistake caused a few pieces of Skylab to land in Australia. Fortunately, there were no injuries.

Mir

COUNTRY: USSR
YEAR OF LAUNCH: 1986
FUN FACT: Lasted more than 15 years in orbit, 3 times longer than its planned lifetime
HISTORY: Mir was the largest space station of its time, and it was the first international space station. It was visited by astronauts from the U.S., the U.K., Japan, and many other countries. The astronauts on Mir performed more than 23,000 science experiments in orbit, and conducted approximately 78 spacewalks.

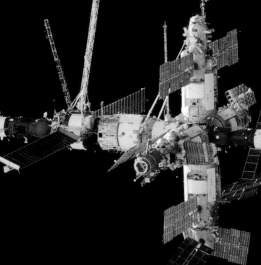

Do you think I can still get a 30-minute pizza delivery?

Salyut 1

COUNTRY: USSR
YEAR OF LAUNCH: 1971
FUN FACT: First habitable space station
HISTORY: The crew of the Soyuz 10 was meant to be the first crew on the space station Salyut 1, but the craft failed to dock. Soyuz 11 successfully docked, and its crew lived on the station for 24 days, experiencing 383 orbits, which at the time was a new space endurance record. Tragically, the entire crew died when the craft malfunctioned upon reentry to Earth. Six more space stations were launched through the Salyut program. The last was Salyut 7, which launched in 1982.

International Space Station (ISS)

COUNTRIES: Many!
YEAR OF LAUNCH: 1998
FUN FACT: Largest space station ever built
HISTORY: The ISS was built with the participation of the U.S., Japan, Canada, and all of the countries in the European Space Agency. Over 115 space flights were involved in the construction of the ISS, and astronauts from more than 18 countries have visited the space station. Even the Olympic torch has visited the ISS and went on a spacewalk with astronauts. There is a wide variety of animals on the space station, including mice, frogs, spiders, and birds.

ROOMMATES WANTED!

Space is harsh and unforgiving, and an astronaut would die almost instantly if he or she went out on a spacewalk unprotected. That's why every astronaut needs a trusty spacesuit to protect him or her from the dangers of space.

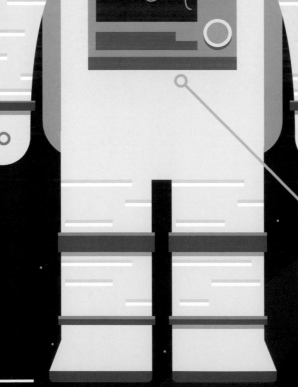

Extravehicular Mobility Unit (EMU)

Spacesuits are not just a fashion statement (although they look fabulous); they are designed to be spacecraft that astronauts wear. Extravehicular means "outside the space vehicle," and mobility unit means that the astronaut uses his or her body to move the suit.

Gold Visor

Ever wondered why the visor of an astronaut's helmet is gold? No, astronauts do not have unusually expensive tastes. The gold tint protects the astronaut from solar radiation.

Drink Tube

Because missions can last many hours, astronauts need to stay hydrated. This tube runs from a drink bag to the astronaut's helmet, so he or she can drink water.

Gloves

Are your hands always cold? Astronauts know how you feel. Space is very cold, so these gloves are equipped with heaters. This allows astronauts to keep their hands at a comfortable temperature as they work in space.

Display and Control Center

Because spacesuits are miniature spacecraft, this box is the control panel for the suit. Astronauts can monitor and control life support functions from this panel. (We wonder if astronauts roll their eyes when someone calls a three-piece suit a "power suit.")

Helmet

Space helmets usually have a light and a camera. The helmet also regulates oxygen pumped in through the life support system attached to the astronaut's suit.

Astronaut Propulsion Unit

If the tethers detach or the astronaut is knocked away from the vehicle, this jetpack is filled with pressurized gas, which will help him or her get back to the craft safely.

Wrist Mirror

This helps the astronaut read the front of the control panel.

Tethers

These straps keep the astronaut secured to the vehicle or space station.

MAG

MAG stands for maximum absorption garment, which is a fancy term for "space diaper." Spacewalking missions can take many hours, and there are no port-a-potties along the way.

PATIENCE IS THE KEY TO GOOD SPACE COMMUNICATION

Do you get annoyed when a friend doesn't reply to your text message right away? Well, that's nothing compared to how long scientists on Earth wait for a signal from different craft in space. These signals travel at the speed of light—which is really fast—but they also travel very far distances. Simply put, if you're a scientist waiting for a signal from most of these locations, you have time to watch a few (or a few hundred) cat videos.

One-way light time = The time it takes a signal to reach a destination if it's travelling at the speed of light.

EARTH TO VOYAGER 1 AND 2
Voyager 1: More than 19 hours and counting!
Voyager 2: 16 hours and counting!

EARTH TO JUNO
48 min 19 s

EARTH TO MOON
1.3 s

EARTH TO CURIOSITY
13 min 48 s

SUN TO EARTH
8 min 20 s

EARTH TO NEW HORIZONS
4 hr 30 min

EARTH TO CASSINI
1 hr 24 minutes
Mission ended: 2017

12 HIT THE PLANET, WIN A PRIZE

MARS!

Between 1960 and 2016, 43 missions launched spacecraft to visit, orbit, or land on Mars. But even with the best plans and the strongest swings, Mars missions reach their target only about half of the time.

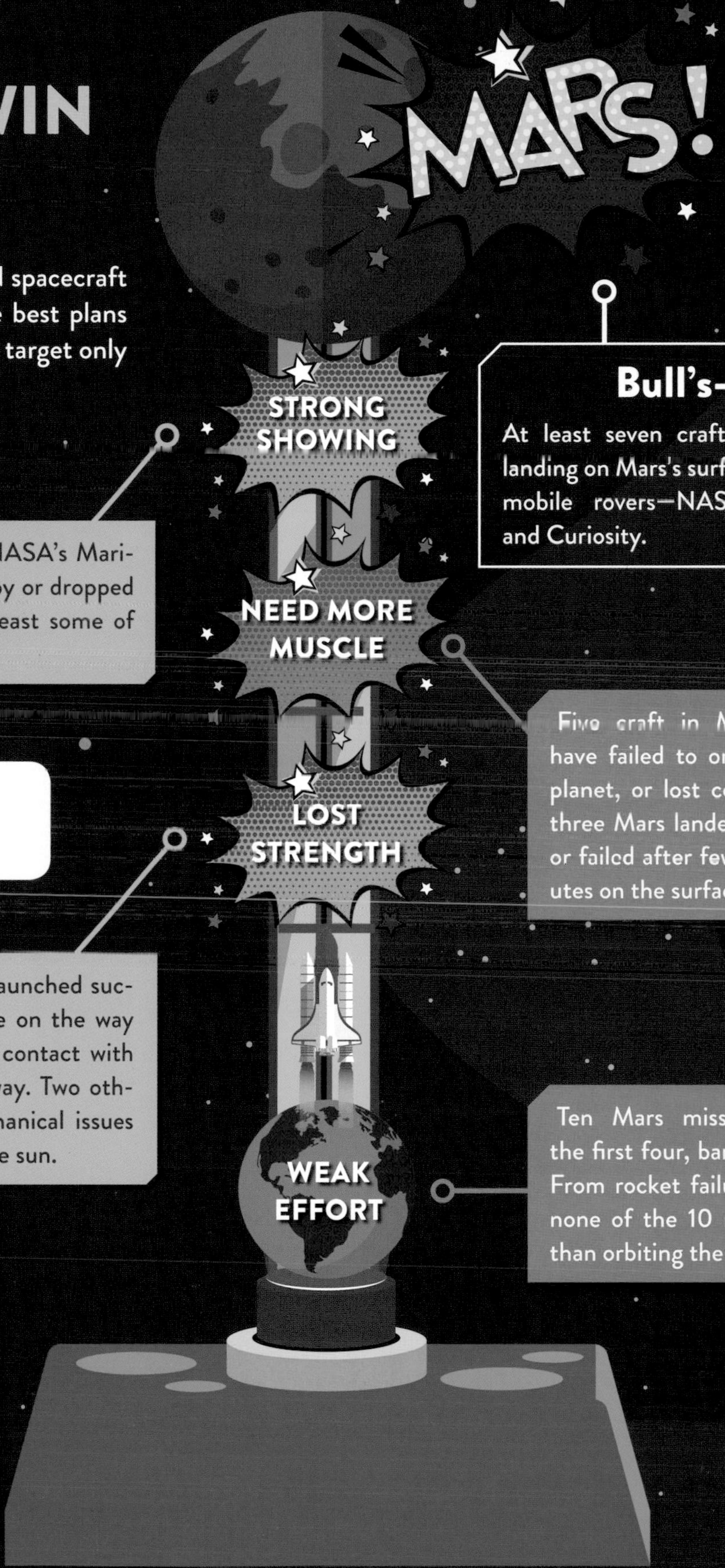

STRONG SHOWING

NEED MORE MUSCLE

LOST STRENGTH

WEAK EFFORT

Bull's-Eye!

At least seven craft have survived a landing on Mars's surface, including two mobile rovers—NASA's Opportunity and Curiosity.

Including the first successful flyby by NASA's Mariner 4 in 1965, 16 spacecraft have flown by or dropped into orbit around Mars, completing at least some of their mission objectives.

Five craft in Mars's backyard have failed to orbit, missed the planet, or lost contact. At least three Mars landers have crashed or failed after fewer than 5 minutes on the surface.

Come on, now! Mars is thataway!

Four spacecraft launched successfully and were on the way to Mars, but lost contact with Earth along the way. Two others suffered mechanical issues and today orbit the sun.

Ten Mars missions, including the first four, barely got started. From rocket failures to crashes, none of the 10 made it farther than orbiting the Earth.

13 WHAT GOES UP MUST LAND, SOMEHOW

Over the years, space scientists have worked out new—and fancier!—ways to land spacecraft and rovers, whether on Earth, the moon, or faraway planets like Mars. Although the landing methods have grown more and more complicated, some have worked better than others.

The first manned spacecraft returning to Earth, including NASA's Mercury, Gemini, and Apollo programs, deployed parachutes to glide the capsules to safe ocean landings, or splashdowns. For some trips, 20 or more naval vessels waited at the ready to pick up the astronauts.

By the 1980s, engineers had designed craft like NASA's space shuttles, which could glide to a landing like an airplane would (if the airplane fell from outer space and had no working engines)—with wheels down on a runway.

In the 1960s, NASA hoped to use its astronauts' piloting experience to land spacecraft using a "Rogallo wing"—a self-inflating paraglider that could be controlled from inside the craft. Despite 10 years of testing, however, the system never made it into a live mission.

NASA's Curiosity rover was too large to land using existing methods, so engineers developed a "sky crane"—basically a rocket-powered extraterrestrial delivery drone—to gently place Curiosity onto the Martian surface.

Looking ahead, space agencies hope someday soon to land reusable rockets on Mars and other bodies (and have successfully tested some on Earth!), allowing for repeat flights, bigger payloads, and perhaps human travel.

Early Mars landers, like Russia's Mars 2 and 3 and NASA's Viking 1 and 2, used parachutes, landing rockets, and aeroshells—hard protective casings cast away during descent—with varying degrees of success.

The moon's low gravity allowed Apollo lunar modules to coast toward the surface, firing landing rockets to bring the craft (and the astronauts inside) to soft landings.

Later missions to Mars added "space airbags," inflatable clusters designed to cushion landings, then deflate to release rovers and other equipment. NASA's Sojourner, Spirit, and Opportunity rovers were all deployed in this way.

THE ANATOMY OF A SPACE SHUTTLE

NASA's Space Shuttle Program ushered in a new era of space travel. For the first time in history, a manned spacecraft could go into space and come back to Earth completely intact so that it could be used again for another mission. The Space Shuttle program ended on July 21, 2011, when the Atlantis orbiter successfully returned to Earth from its final mission.

Height: 184 ft (56 m)

External Tank

A shuttle needed a lot of power to travel fast enough to escape Earth's gravity. Almost all of the fuel in this tank was burned up within 8 minutes and 30 seconds. Ten seconds later, this tank separated from the orbiter and burned up in the atmosphere.

Solid Rocket Boosters

True to their name, these rockets boosted the shuttle upward at a high enough speed to escape Earth's gravity. The rocket boosters dropped off the craft 126 seconds after liftoff, and they were recovered to use again for another flight.

Orbiter

The orbiter carried the crew. It landed back on Earth just like an airplane.

Today, you can visit the existing orbiters in these locations:

- **Atlantis:** Kennedy Space Center, FL
- **Endeavour:** California Science Center, Los Angeles, CA
- **Discovery:** Udvar-Hazy Center, Chantilly, VA
- **Enterprise:** Intrepid Sea, Air & Space Museum, New York City, NY

ENTERPRISE

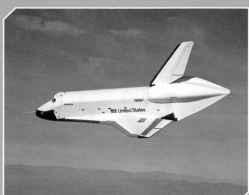

DISTANCE TRAVELED IN SPACE: 0 miles (0 km)

NUMBER OF SPACE FLIGHTS: 0

FACTS:

- First space shuttle built (1976)
- When it rolled out of the factory, it was greeted by the cast from *Star Trek*
- Never flew in space because it was used as a test vehicle

COLUMBIA

DISTANCE TRAVELED IN SPACE: 121.6 million miles (195.7 million km)

NUMBER OF SPACE FLIGHTS: 28

FACTS:

- First space shuttle in space (1981)
- Named after a Boston sailing vessel used in the 1700s
- Crashed on February 1, 2003, killing all seven crew members

CHALLENGER

DISTANCE TRAVELED IN SPACE: 23.6 million miles (37.9 million km)

NUMBER OF SPACE FLIGHTS: 10

FACTS:

- In 1983, Challenger crew conducted the first spacewalk of the Space Shuttle Program
- Christa McAuliffe was chosen to join the crew to be the first teacher in space
- All crew members were killed in the 1986 Challenger explosion

DISCOVERY

DISTANCE TRAVELED IN SPACE: 148.2 million miles (238.5 million km)

NUMBER OF FLIGHTS: 39

FACTS:

- World record holder for most flights into space by a single craft
- Astronauts aboard Discovery deployed the Hubble telescope
- Last mission flew in 2011

ATLANTIS

DISTANCE TRAVELED IN SPACE: 120.7 million miles (194.2 million km)

NUMBER OF FLIGHTS: 32

FACTS:

- Named for a sailing ship that operated in Maryland
- Launched the Galileo probe to Jupiter
- Final flight of the shuttle program in 2011

ENDEAVOUR

DISTANCE TRAVELED IN SPACE: 122.9 million miles (197.9 million km)

NUMBER OF FLIGHTS: 25

FACTS:

- Youngest of the space shuttle fleet
- Named by students during a contest held by NASA
- One Endeavour crew saved the Hubble telescope by repairing a problem that was causing blurry images

HEADING INWARD

Exploring our neighbors Venus and Mercury could help scientists understand a bit more about how the rocky planets formed. Here are the some of the missions that have visited these two hotheaded planets.

Venera Missions

- Soviet, 1961–1984
- Consisted of 16 missions
- Venera 7 was the first probe to land on Venus

Mariner 5

- NASA, 1967
- Designed to use radio waves to collect information about Venus's atmosphere

Pioneer Venus 1 and 2

- NASA, 1978
- Consisted of two craft—an orbiter and a landing probe
- Its goal was to map the surface of Venus

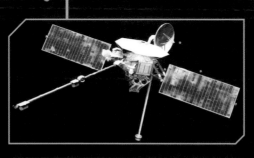

1970

1980

1960

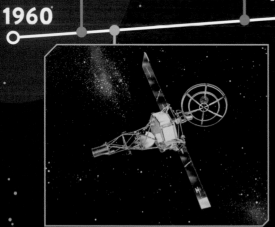

Mariner 2

- NASA, 1962
- First craft to successfully visit another planet

Mariner 10

- NASA, 1973
- First craft to reach Mercury
- First craft to use the gravity of one planet (Venus) to reach another planet (Mercury)

Vega 1 and 2

- Soviet, 1984
- Also conducted a flyby of Halley's Comet

MERCURY

Venus sure is popular!

VENUS

Parker Solar Probe

- NASA, 2018
- Completed flyby of Venus in October 2018
- Plans to fly right through the sun's corona, the outer level of the sun's atmosphere

Venus Express

- European Space Agency, 2005
- Designed to study the interaction between Venus's upper atmosphere and solar wind

Magellan

- NASA, 1989
- First U.S. mission to create high-resolution global map of Venus using radar

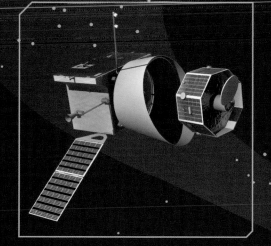

1990

2000

2010

PRESENT

MESSENGER

- NASA, 2004
- First craft to orbit Mercury

Akatsuki (Venus Climate Orbiter)

- Japan, 2010
- Failed to achieve orbit in 2010, but successfully achieved orbit in 2015 (If at first you don't succeed . . . try again!)

BepiColombo

- European Space Agency and Japanese Aerospace Exploration Agency, 2018
- Europe's first mission to Mercury, the least explored planet in the solar system.

25

16 IT'S COMPUTATION, NOT A COMPETITION

It takes powerful computers and fancy calculations to send a craft into space. But the computers that actually go into space aboard those craft are often relatively puny. It's more important for those devices to be shockproof, freeze-proof, radiation-resistant, low-heat, long-lasting, and reliable. Here's how a few famous spacefaring computers compare to earthbound tech:

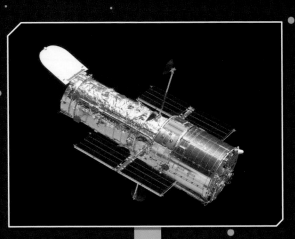

In 1969, the Apollo Guidance Computer (AGC) was state of the art, and safely delivered the first astronauts to the moon and back. The AGC's operating system wouldn't freeze or crash—but it had just 64 KB of memory and simpler electronics than a modern "smart" toaster.

NASA's Voyager 1 and 2 probes were designed with redundant systems for safety—but 1977 technology. That means they had only about 170 KB of memory combined and a network speed of 160 bits per second (about 300,000 times slower than the average U.S. home internet connection).

In 1990, the Hubble Space Telescope launched with an 8-bit, 110-pound DF-224 computer, which was upgraded (in space!) in 1993 with Intel 386 chips, and in 1999 with 486 processors. Today, Hubble still runs on hardware best known for supporting Windows 95.

Awesome Space Tech

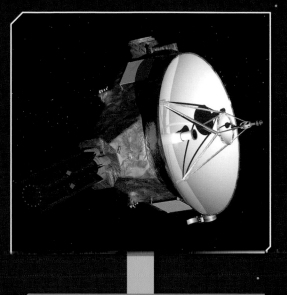

NASA's Orion craft is being tested now to someday deliver astronauts to Mars. And the computers inside? Safe, reliable, dependable chips, first made in 2002. Apple used the same CPUs in the first iMacs, but moved to faster chips in 2006—the year before the first iPhone.

The New Horizons probe wowed us in 2015 with up-close views of Pluto—but don't forget, New Horizons was launched back in 2006. At the time, it was fitted with the same computer chip used in the original Sony PlayStation, a MIPS R3000. Game over, man!

The space shuttles employed more modern technology, but still valued reliability more than raw power in the computer systems. When the shuttle Atlantis took the fleet's last trip in 2011, it launched with a flight computer with less than 1% of the power of an Xbox 360 console.

I dunno. Did you check your Wi-Fi router?

THE WEIRDNESS OF JUNO

The Juno mission launched in 2011, and NASA has extended the mission through July 2021. Juno is one of the most impressive—and weirdest—spacecraft ever built. Here are some of the reasons why:

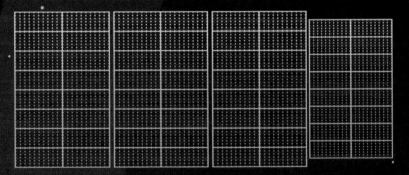

Juno has the biggest solar arrays of any craft launched into space! Juno needs panels this large so that the craft can get energy even when available light is limited.

DANGER! RADIATION!

Juno is built to withstand the strong radiation created by Jupiter's ginormous magnetosphere. Many of Juno's internal electronics are covered in thick titanium to protect them from radiation damage, and Juno's external stargazer camera has a thick protective covering that makes it 4 times heavier than most other stargazers.

Length of adult Siberian tiger:
10 ft (3.2 m)

Length of one Juno Panel:

JUPITER'S MAGNETOSPHERE

In 2016, Juno surpassed the Rosetta spacecraft to become the farthest traveled solar-powered spacecraft ever built!

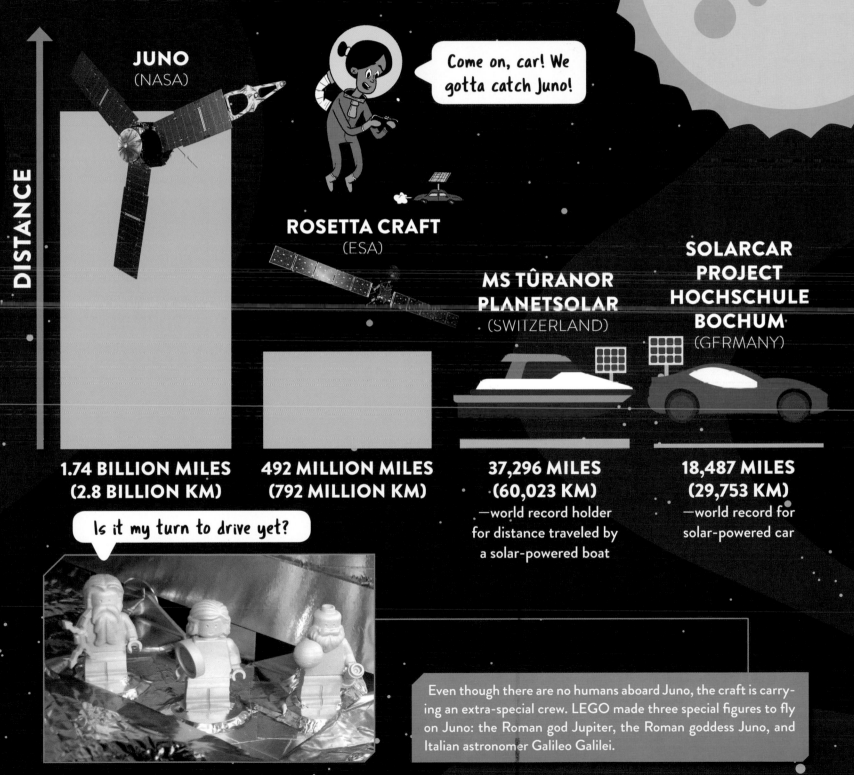

DISTANCE

JUNO
(NASA)

Come on, car! We gotta catch Juno!

ROSETTA CRAFT
(ESA)

MS TÛRANOR PLANETSOLAR
(SWITZERLAND)

SOLARCAR PROJECT HOCHSCHULE BOCHUM
(GERMANY)

**1.74 BILLION MILES
(2.8 BILLION KM)**

**492 MILLION MILES
(792 MILLION KM)**

**37,296 MILES
(60,023 KM)**
—world record holder
for distance traveled by
a solar-powered boat

**18,487 MILES
(29,753 KM)**
—world record for
solar-powered car

Is it my turn to drive yet?

Even though there are no humans aboard Juno, the craft is carrying an extra-special crew. LEGO made three special figures to fly on Juno: the Roman god Jupiter, the Roman goddess Juno, and Italian astronomer Galileo Galilei.

18 THE ORIGIN OF (SPACE) SPECIES

When humans venture into space, we're rarely alone—and we weren't the first to go. Since the 1940s, we've been sending (or bringing) plant and animal species into space. Species like these:

Most plants grown in space are the subjects of scientific experiments. But in 2015, the "Veggie" growth system aboard the ISS allowed astronauts to munch on space-grown romaine lettuce salads.

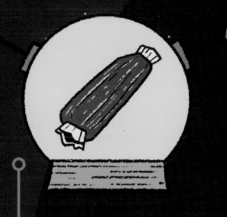

Veggies like onions and cabbages first made it to space aboard the Soviet craft Salyut 1 in 1971. In 2012, a zucchini grown on the ISS blogged about its trip (with some help from NASA astronaut Don Pettit).

The first space spiders made the trip in 1973, to answer the question of whether spiders can spin webs in the weightlessness of space. Spidernauts Arabella and Anita proved that, yes, they can!

The first animals sent to outer space were fruit flies, launched 68 miles up aboard a V-2 rocket in 1947. After the rocket parachuted back to Earth, all of the flies were recovered alive.

In 1963, French scientists wanted to make Felix the first cat in space—but before launch, Felix ran away! He was replaced by Félicette, who made the trip and returned to Earth safely.

In 2007, ESA astronauts exposed samples of living (but dormant) microscopic tardigrades (also known as water bears) to the vacuum of space for 10 days. When revived later, most tardigrades survived!

The first monkey to enter space (Albert II) made the trip in 1949, and more than 30 monkeys have followed since. That includes macaques, squirrel monkeys, pig-tailed monkeys, and chimpanzees.

Sure, but . . . where's the USS Swinetrek?

Humans' best friends have been part of space travel since the 1950s. Russian pup Laika became the first living creature to orbit Earth in 1957 on Sputnik 2, and two other Soviet space doggies orbited for 22 days in 1966.

JUST WHAT THE SPACE DOCTOR ORDERED

Astronauts on the International Space Station conduct research that may one day help humans stay safe and healthy during extended space travel. Much of this research also helps to fuel medical advancements for people living on Earth's surface.

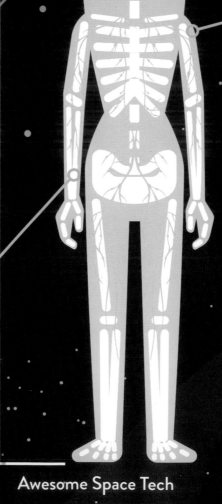

Build-a-Protein Workshop

Astronauts have discovered that the microgravity of space is the perfect environment to build complicated proteins that can be used to develop new medications for serious diseases.

The Rise of the Robotic Surgeon Machines

Robotic arms that are used to perform vehicle maintenance on the ISS have inspired the design of the neuroArm, a robotic arm used to perform complicated brain surgeries.

Building Stronger Bones

The microgravity in space can be rough on an astronaut's bones. In fact, an astronaut can lose 1%–2% of his or her bone density during a 30-day mission. Studying the bones of ISS astronauts has helped scientists understand the risks of osteoporosis—a serious disease that causes people to develop brittle bones as they age.

Got My Eye (Tracker) On You

Technology used to track astronauts' eye movement in space is now used by surgeons when they perform laser eye surgery to correct a patient's vision.

Take That, You Nasty Germs!

Some species of bacteria develop dangerous genetic mutations in space that allow them to reproduce rapidly or infect humans more easily. Studying these bacteria on the ISS could lead to the development of better vaccines.

De-muddying the Waters

There are no bottled water vending machines in space, so the water purification machines on the ISS are designed to be reliable and portable. Similar machines also supply clean water to people in regions on Earth that lack proper water treatment or have limited access to clean water due to natural disasters.

20 NEVER KNOCK AN OPPORTUNITY

After landing safely in January 2004, NASA's Mars rover Opportunity was only planned to operate for 90 days—but it was still active in June 2018. What if other things lasted more than 58 times longer than expected?

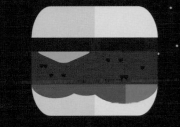

The "5-second rule" would be nearly
5 MINUTES LONG.

It would take
ALMOST 5 DAYS
to watch the original *Star Wars* movie.

The 12 days of Chistmas would last
NEARLY 2 YEARS.

OPPORTUNITY ROVER: 5,000+ DAYS!

TIME

SOCIAL NETWORKING ON MARS

The Mars rovers have complicated—and ingenious—methods of communicating with Earth. This is how the Curiosity rover chats with us.

The Deep Space Network is made up of powerful antennae that are positioned at different points around the world. Multiple antennae ensure that as the Earth rotates, we can still take Curiosity's call.

Most of our transmissions from Curiosity come through one of the Mars orbiters. This occurs because Curiosity is not always within sight of Earth, but it is almost always within sight of one of these orbiters. Also, it requires less energy for Curiosity to send a signal to a nearby orbiter than it does to send one all of the way to Earth.

THE TITAN OF TELESCOPES

Even after more than 25 years of service, the Hubble telescope is still a jaw-dropping feat of human innovation. So, you can imagine why scientists are excited about the James Webb telescope, which is designed to be even more powerful than the Hubble. Here are some of the ways the two telescopes compare.

JAMES WEBB

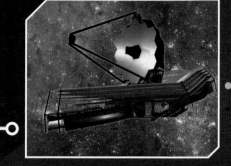

James Webb will orbit with the Earth around the sun, but it will not directly orbit the Earth like Hubble does. It will also be so far away from Earth that it cannot be repaired or serviced by astronauts.

HUBBLE

A Widescreen View

Its humongous mirror will allow the James Webb telescope to collect and analyze data from a much larger field of view than the Hubble telescope has.

Covering Our Electromagnetic Bases

The James Webb telescope will primarily process infrared light and some visible light waves, which will allow us to capture data that the Hubble telescope cannot.

2.4 meters (7.8 feet)
Hubble mirror

6.5 meters (21.3 feet)
Webb mirror

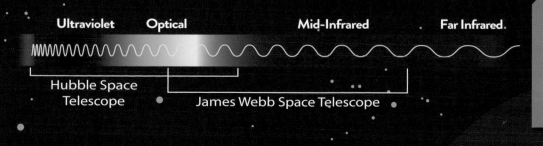

Ultraviolet   Optical   Mid-Infrared   Far Infrared

Hubble Space Telescope

James Webb Space Telescope

Time Traveling

Because James Webb will primarily interpret infrared radiation, it will be able to see older stars, galaxies, and other space objects than Hubble can. This will allow scientists to have a better understanding of how this crazy, amazing universe began.

SIX SPACE 'SCOPES SCANNING THE SKIES FOR SCIENCE...

Although there are many powerful telescopes on Earth, the best way to explore the mysteries of space is to be floating in it, above the interference of the atmosphere. Below are some of today's most advanced space telescopes and the important research they perform.

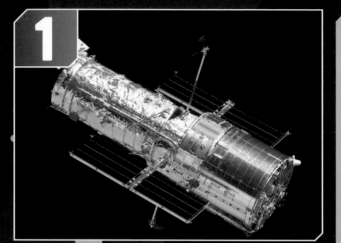

Chandra X-Ray Observatory

Since 1999, the Chandra X-Ray Observatory has studied black holes, supernovas, quasars and other cosmic X-ray sources, some of them billions of light-years away. Chandra can produce images 25 times sharper than the next-best X-ray telescope.

Hubble Space Telescope

The Hubble Space Telescope was launched in 1990, and is still scanning space in ultraviolet, visual, and near-infrared wavelengths. Hubble has been used to study star formation, star deaths, black holes, galaxy formation, and much, much more.

Spitzer Space Telescope

Covering infrared wavelengths that are blocked on Earth's surface by the atmosphere, the Spitzer Space Telescope, launched in 2003, can see through dense clouds of gas and dust that visible light cannot penetrate, opening whole new areas of the sky for exploration.

The Hubble, Chandra, and Spitzer telescopes are three of NASA's four "Great Observatories," designed to explore the cosmos across the spectrum. (The fourth, the Compton Gamma Ray Observatory, was de-orbited in June 2000.)

Fermi Gamma-Ray Space Telescope

NASA's Fermi Gamma-Ray Space Telescope, launched in 2008, detects the highest-energy wavelengths, the gamma rays. By studying these, we can learn more about supermassive black holes, cosmic rays, and other high-energy phenomena.

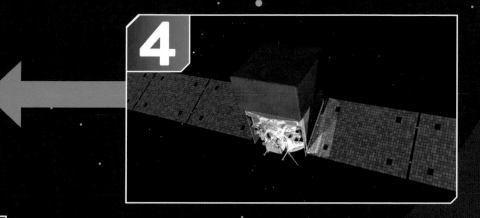

4

5

Gaia

The mission of the Gaia spacecraft, launched by ESA in 2013, is to map the Milky Way more precisely than ever before. Gaia will observe one billion stars 70 times each, resulting in the most richly detailed physical map of our galaxy to date.

Kepler

The Kepler mission, launched by NASA in 2009, is all about exoplanets. Kepler can detect tiny dips in the brightness of faraway stars, which indicate planets orbiting those stars and passing in front. As of 2018, Kepler discovered more than 2,300 confirmed exoplanets.

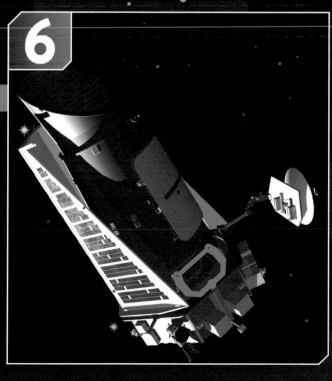

6

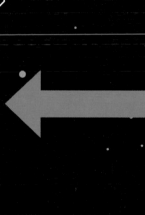

You can see all that? I think I need new glasses.

24 ...AND FOUR FAR-FLUNG FLYERS FOR THE FUTURE

While today's telescopes analyze the energy given off by distant stars in the past, astronomers are directing their energy toward the future. Below are a few space telescopes recently launched or planned to launch in the coming years and gaze ever deeper into the cosmos.

1

Transiting Exoplanet Survey Satellite

The MIT-designed Transiting Exoplanet Survey Satellite (TESS) launched in April 2018, and should soon surpass Kepler's exoplanet-hunting capabilities. If all goes to plan, TESS will cover 400 times more sky than Kepler's survey, and focus on Earth-sized exoplanets.

James Webb Space Telescope

Launching in 2021, NASA's James Webb Space Telescope is a replacement for Hubble—and then some. The Webb will have a larger collection mirror, much sharper imaging, better infrared range, and a higher orbit allowing for longer data collections.

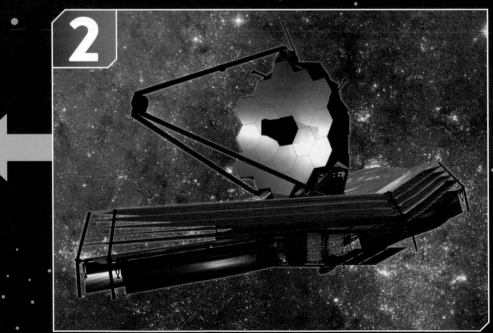

2

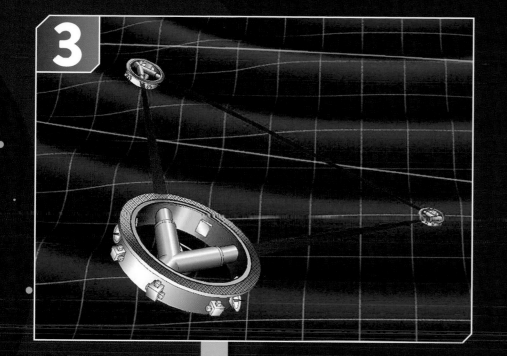

3

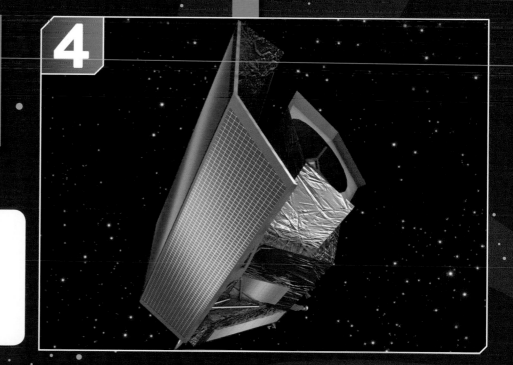

4

Euclid

Scheduled for 2019 or 2020, ESA's Euclid telescope is designed to explore the virtually undetectable: the mysterious dark energy and dark matter. By closely studying the universe's expansion, scientists hope Euclid will shine some light on these cosmic question marks.

Laser Interferometer Space Antenna

ESA hopes to launch the Laser Interferometer Space Antenna (LISA) around 2034. Made up of three craft orbiting in a wide triangle, LISA will detect gravitational waves, shivers in space-time caused by colliding black holes, and other monstrously energetic events.

What are we waiting for? Let's get launching, already!

FALLING IS THE HOTTEST PART

Getting a craft into space is hard enough—but if you want that craft to land again (on Earth or elsewhere), you may have to deal with a trickier problem: intense heat caused by friction of molecules in the atmosphere hitting the craft at high speed. This heat could tear apart or even melt most spacecraft—so you need a heat shield.

The Mars Science Laboratory (MSL) that landed the Curiosity rover on Mars used an ablative carbon fiber-based heat shield substance called PICA, which has also been used on craft landing on Earth.

For future Mars missions, scientists are working on new systems of inflatable heat shields. To survive the Martian atmosphere, these will have to withstand temperatures up to 2,300° F and winds more than 25,000 mph!

Some early missions, like NASA's Apollo modules, used epoxy resin heat shields that were ablative, meaning the material vaporized as the atmosphere heated it (up to 5,000° F).

Whew! It's like a suana up here!

Other craft, like the space shuttles, were fitted with heat sinks—materials like silica or carbon fiber able to absorb massive amounts of heat—keeping the craft and crew above safe and (relatively) cool.

THE LITTLE SATELLITES THAT COULD (AND ALREADY DO!)

26

Most satellites are large and heavy, but a new wave of tiny low-mass satellites is taking low-orbit space by storm. Cheaper to build, easier to launch, and more quickly replaceable than traditional satellites, these scaled-down orbiters show that good satellites can come in (very) small packages.

Nanosatellites have masses between 1–10 kg (2.2–22 lb.), including the 1U CubeSat, a cube of about 10 cm per side, which can be linked with others to create bigger satellites. As of 2018, more than 500 nanosatellites were already in orbit.

Even smaller, picosatellites are between 0.1 and 1 kg (0.22–2.2 lb.) in mass. Some, like the PocketQube, can be configured by "do-it-yourself" users keen to send their own teeny machines into space.

Smaller still, femtosatellites are under 0.1kg (0.22 lb.) in mass. Like their nano and pico cousins, femtosatellites can "swarm," or coordinate with others in large groups, to collectively provide powerful satellite capabilities.

I can't tell where the satellites end and the space dust begins!

A SPACE CAMP RIGHT IN OUR BACKYARDS

Before spacecraft and astronauts are sent into space, they go through a series of tests on the ground to make sure they are ready for the trip. Here are some notable past and present test sites.

Cinder Lake Crater Fields

In the late 1960s, NASA used dynamite to create large crater fields that Apollo 11 astronauts Neil Armstrong, Buzz Aldrin, and Michael Collins used to train for the first manned moon landing. Here, the astronauts learned how to take rock samples, drive the lunar rover, use communication equipment, and survive on the moon.

Black Point Lava Flow Desert

This is the site of NASA's Desert RATS (Research and Technology Studies) programs. Engineers can test out their vehicles, robots, spacesuits, and communication systems to see if they can survive the harsh winds, dry climate, and high temperatures of the region. This helps engineers determine if their equipment will survive the extreme conditions in space.

Mauna Loa

In early 2017, a small group of scientists entered a small dome where they were isolated from the rest of the world for 8 months. This research was part of several similar studies conducted by NASA to determine how isolation can mentally affect astronauts on a longer space trip. The scientists had to wear spacesuits when they went outside, and they could only eat nonperishable food and vegetables they grew in the dome.

Ellington Air Force Base

The swimming pool at this site was used by Neil Armstrong and his crew to practice exiting their landing capsule.

FLAGSTAFF, AZ

HOUSTON, TX

KEY LARGO, FL

MAUNA LOA, HI

NORTHERN CHILE

Aquarius Underwater Laboratory

Nemo is more than just an animated fish to astronauts. NEEMO stands for NASA Extreme Environment Mission Operations, and it is the world's only underwater laboratory. Astronauts come to live here for up to 3 weeks at a time. The extreme conditions under the ocean train them for space travel. For instance, they learn how to maneuver in microgravity by using the natural buoyancy of the ocean.

Askja Caldera

In the mid-1960s, several Apollo astronauts visited this site for moon geology training. Dr. Elbert A. King, the Apollo program geologist, stated, "We took one of our best field trips to Iceland. If you want to go to a place on Earth that looks like the moon, central Iceland should be high on your list, as it beautifully displays volcanic geology with virtually no vegetation cover."

NORTHERN ICELAND

SARDINIA, ITALY

Sardinia, Italy

This was the site of the CAVES 2011 Mission conducted by the European Space Agency. The mission involved five astronauts living and working in a dark, isolated cave for over one week to train for a mission to another planet or moon.

Atacama Desert

Zoë is the name of a NASA robot prototype that is designed to detect evidence for life on other planets. If Zoë accurately detects life in this desert, then it's possible that it can accurately detect any life on Mars.

McMurdo Complex

In January 2008, NASA engineers tested prototypes for inflatable lunar housing that could be used by astronauts for longer stays on the moon.

ANTARCTICA

THE FUTURE'S SO BRIGHT, WE'RE GONNA NEED SHIELDS

Space radiation is a problem. Around Earth, our planet's atmosphere and magnetic field protect us (and nearby satellites) from most radiation. Scientists shield space probes and landers traveling out into the solar system. But if we want to travel to Mars—or beyond—ourselves, we'll have to find ways to protect astronauts and space colonists from solar and cosmic radiation.

One proposed way to add shielding against cosmic rays is to line the walls of spacecraft with material already on board— water, food, or even the astronauts' waste. The extra material would "catch" more cosmic rays, but would gradually be used, recycled, or disposed of.

Cosmic radiation is made up of high-energy particles produced by faraway supernovae, quasars, and other sources. These "cosmic rays" often pass through solid matter at near-light speed—but when they don't, they can do serious damage to computers, craft, and our DNA.

Because human astronauts would be the most precious cargo, scientists are working on custom-fitted vests made of layers of protective material for astronauts to wear. (For the entire trip. Hopefully, it matches the rest of their wardrobe.)

Unlike Earth, Mars doesn't have a magnetic field to protect against cosmic radiation. Mars's atmosphere is also much thinner than Earth's, allowing more solar radiation to reach the surface. Proposed habitats for Mars explorers are heavily shielded—or even underground.

The sun emits many types of radiation, including ultra-violet (UV) and relatively low-energy particles. These can typically be blocked by spacecraft walls—but the craft must also be designed to shield radiation from unpredictable solar flares and coronal mass ejections (CMEs).

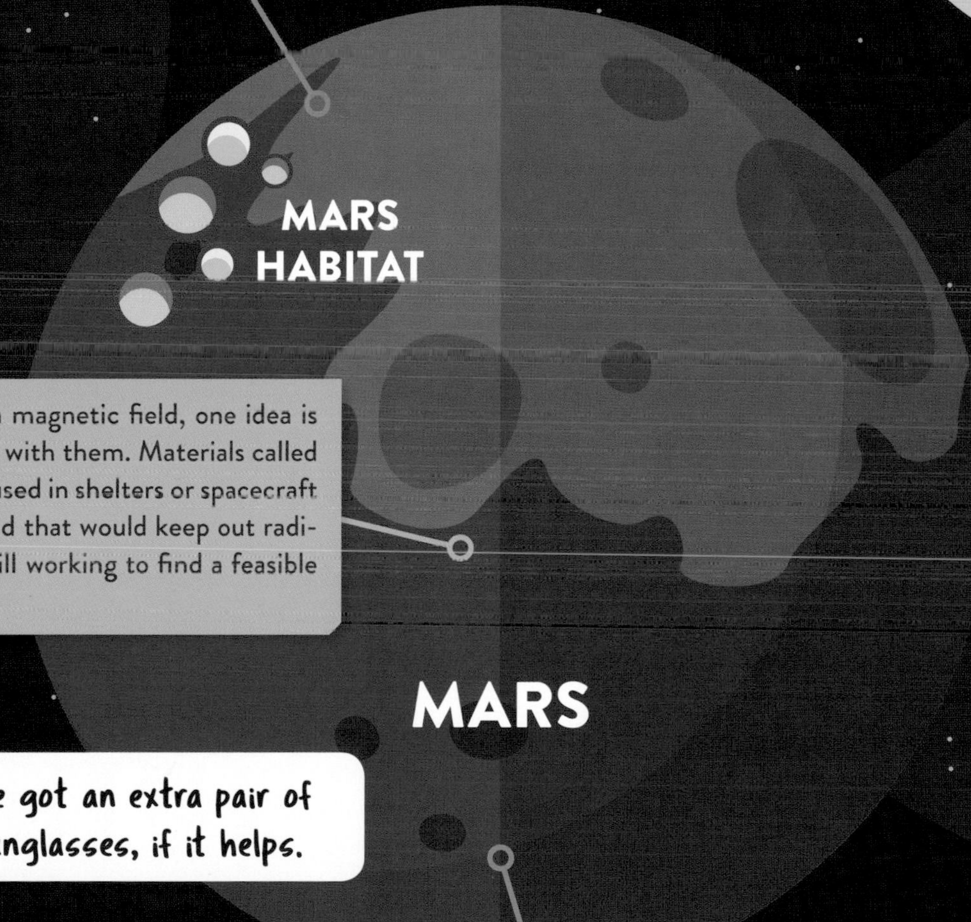

MARS HABITAT

Because Mars is missing a magnetic field, one idea is for astronauts to bring one with them. Materials called superconductors could be used in shelters or spacecraft to generate a magnetic field that would keep out radiation—but scientists are still working to find a feasible solution.

MARS

I've got an extra pair of sunglasses, if it helps.

THE SUN

Someday, we could even give Mars a magnetic field of its own. In 2017, scientists ran computer simulations to explore the effects of a powerful magnetic shield put into orbit around Mars. The results were encouraging—but we're many years away from the technology needed.

Earthlings rely on satellites for everything from making a phone call to using our GPS devices. Different types of satellites are designed to have different types of orbits.

Lagrange Points Satellites

Distance: 1.5 million km from Earth
Examples: James Webb Telescope, Solar and Heliospheric Observatory satellite (SOHO)
Description: These satellites do not orbit the Earth, but they are at a distance that allows them to orbit with the Earth around the sun. These distant satellites are useful for monitoring solar activity and observing distant galaxies.

Medium-Earth Orbit: Semi-Synchronous

Distance above Earth's surface: 20,200 km
Examples: GPS satellites
Description: These satellites have near-circular orbits and complete one orbit every 12 hours. For complete coverage of GPS services all over the globe, constellations of satellites must be used.

Molniya Orbit

Distance above Earth's surface: Varies at different points during the orbit due to high eccentricity
Example: Molniya-series satellite system (Russia)
Description: These satellites complete one orbit every 12 hours, but due to the orbit shape, most of the time is spent above one hemisphere. Molniya satellites are named after Russian communication satellites that used similar orbits for telecommunication. Because there are short periods when a satellite will orbit on the other side of the Earth, multiple satellites must be used to ensure complete coverage.

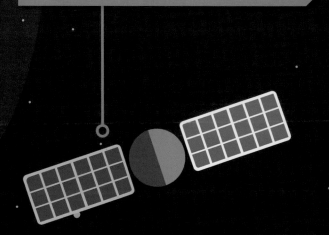

Low-Earth Orbit (LEO)

Distance above Earth's surface: 160–2,000 km
Examples: International Space Station, space shuttles, Hubble Telescope, CryoSat-2
Description: LEO satellites are used for craft that carry or require frequent servicing by astronauts. They usually complete one orbit of the Earth in 84–127 minutes. CryoSat-2 orbits the poles. Polar-orbiting satellites are often used to monitor climate and other environmental changes at the poles.

High-Earth Orbit: Geosynchronous

Distance above Earth's surface: 35,786 km

Example: GOES

Description: Satellites move slower the farther they are from Earth. Geosynchronous satellites move at the speed of the Earth's rotation. This makes them especially useful for monitoring weather and telecommunications because they appear to stay stationary over one point in space. Due to their distance, these satellites require a lot of energy to maintain their orbits.

COMMUNICATIONS FROM HOME BASE

Although humans have sent some pretty impressive craft into space, we also have mighty instruments on the ground to communicate with distant spacecraft or to listen for any signs of extraterrestrial life.

THE STANFORD DISH
150 ft (46 m)

LOCATION: United States

PURPOSES: Studying distant galaxies; communicating with satellites and Voyager craft

EFFELSBERG 100-M RADIO TELESCOPE
328 ft (100 m)

LOCATION: Germany

PURPOSE: Studying pulsars and distant galaxies

ARECIBO OBSERVATORY
1,001 ft (305 m)

LOCATION: Puerto Rico

PURPOSES: Tracking asteroids and exoplanets; looking for signs of extraterrestrial life

FIVE-HUNDRED-METER APERTURE SPHERICAL TELESCOPE
1,650 FT (503 M)

LOCATION: China

PURPOSE: Listening for signs of distant life

DIAMETER →

THE GRAVITY CIRCUS

Our rockets can push spacecraft into space near Earth, but to reach faraway planets and moons, those craft need some serious speed. They gain that speed by whipping close around planets, letting gravity "slingshot" them away in a new direction. Some of the flight paths get pretty complicated—like the trip the Cassini probe made to reach Saturn.

Venus Flyby —Apr. 1998

Venus Flyby (again!)—Jun. 1999

Launch—Oct. 1997

Whew!

Earth Flyby —Aug. 1999

Hey, what took you so long?

To Saturn or bust!

Jupiter Flyby —Dec. 2000

49

 **RUNNING RINGS AROUND SATURN**

The Cassini probe had 12 different scientific instruments onboard, which paved the way for many new discoveries about Saturn. Here are some of the most interesting things we learned about Saturn from Cassini.

SATURN

You Complete Me

In 2004, Cassini observed two giant storms on Saturn merging to become one giant storm. This was only the second time in history that this phenomenon was observed. The first was by Voyager in 1981.

Congratulations! It's (Possibly) a Moon!

One of the most unexpected discoveries by Cassini was the possible birth of a new moon on the outer edge of Cassini's A ring. The small icy object is nicknamed Peggy, and it may help scientists understand how some of Saturn's moons formed from material in the rings.

PEGGY

F = Fast and Furious

If you're a daredevil, you'd be right at home in Saturn's F ring, which scientists believe is the most chaotic ring in the solar system. The structure of the ring is constantly changing, and new structures form and disappear within hours or days. Cassini discovered mini-jets, which are small objects that pass through the F ring, leaving glittery streaks.

RHEA

Breathe It In

Cassini collected oxygen molecules in the atmosphere of Saturn's moon Rhea. This was the first time oxygen molecules were collected by a spacecraft in an atmosphere other than Earth's.

You Can Never Have Too Much Bling

Saturn has the largest ring system in the solar system, but there are even more rings than we once thought. Thanks to Cassini's up-close look on the planet, scientists spotted faint rings between the bright inner rings of Saturn and between the more distant G and E rings.

Seven New Friend Requests

Cassini spotted seven previously undiscovered moons orbiting Saturn, which include the three tiny moons, Methone, Pallene, and Anthe. These three moons range from 1 to 3 miles in diameter (1.6–4.8 km).

TITAN

Even More Friend Requests?

Cassini released the Huygens lander, which landed on the surface of Titan. Even though the probe died a few hours later, it did find evidence of prebiotic chemistry on the surface. Prebiotic means "before life," which means there is a potential for life on the surface of Titan.

Don't Blow Your Top

During its mission, Cassini found 101 sites where geysers of liquid water erupt on the surface of Saturn's moon Enceladus. The water from the geysers likely comes from a large ocean underneath Enceladus's icy surface. Cassini found evidence that this ocean may have hydrothermal vents, which are warm and cozy regions where life could potentially be found.

ENCELADUS

Giving Mixed Signals

Scientists used radio waves from Jupiter to estimate how long it took the planet to rotate, but Cassini discovered that Saturn's radio waves are much, much weirder. The northern and southern hemispheres send out different signals, and there are also seasonal differences in the radio signals. This means that Saturn's rotation is still a bit of a mystery.

CASSINI

33 A GINORMOUS JUMBLE OF JUNK

Since humans first launched objects into space, we've also been accumulating debris in orbit, or "space junk." From defunct satellites, to used rockets, to small metal debris, there's a lot of junk up there—and that can be a real problem.

In orbit, there are around 20,000 objects larger than a softball, about 500,000 objects larger than a marble, and millions smaller than that. Because they all orbit at speeds of up to 17,500 mph, even a collision with a fleck of paint can cause serious damage!

Collisions do happen in space, occasionally damaging satellites and spacecraft—but not all bumps with space junk are random. In 2007, Chinese scientists destroyed an old weather satellite with a missile, adding 3,000 more bits of debris to space.

Space agencies have agreed that defunct satellites should be designed to fall out of orbit back to Earth when they've stopped working—but not all satellites are built that way. In 2015, less than two-thirds were designed to take a final plunge.

With thousands more satellites—including microsatellites, just a few inches on each side—planned to launch in the next few years, the space junk problem is growing. Scientists hope to thin the debris someday by grabbing, netting, or melting it.

34 THE WEIRDEST LOST AND FOUND

Some of the junk that ends up in space includes items that were dumped accidentally or purposely by spacewalking astronauts. Here are some of the weirdest.

On July 12, 2006, spacewalker Piers Sellers accidentally dropped a spatula that he was using to test exterior heating tiles. Four months later, Sellers received a note from the North American Aerospace Defense Command stating that the spatula reentered Earth's atmosphere and burned up over the Atlantic.

On November 10, 2008, astronaut Heidemarie Stefanyshyn-Piper accidentally dropped her $100,000 tool bag during a spacewalking mission on the ISS. She let go of the bag when she was cleaning up the mess from a leaky grease gun. The bag orbited Earth for a few months until it reentered the atmosphere on August 3, 2009.

Russian ISS astronauts had a worn-out spacesuit that they couldn't bring back to Earth, so they turned it into a satellite. Called SuitSat-1, the spacesuit was released into orbit in 2006 with the hopes that it could provide data that would help scientists build better spacesuits. Unfortunately, Suitsat-1 stopped transmitting to Earth after only two orbits. It eventually fell out of orbit and burned up in Earth's atmosphere just a year later.

In September 2009, sky watchers noticed a beautiful, sparkling trail across the night sky. Was it the northern lights . . . an unexpected celestial event? Nope! It was astronaut pee. The space shuttle Discovery had just dumped its wastewater into space. The urine froze into sparkling crystals, giving the sky-gazers on Earth a "wee" spectacle.

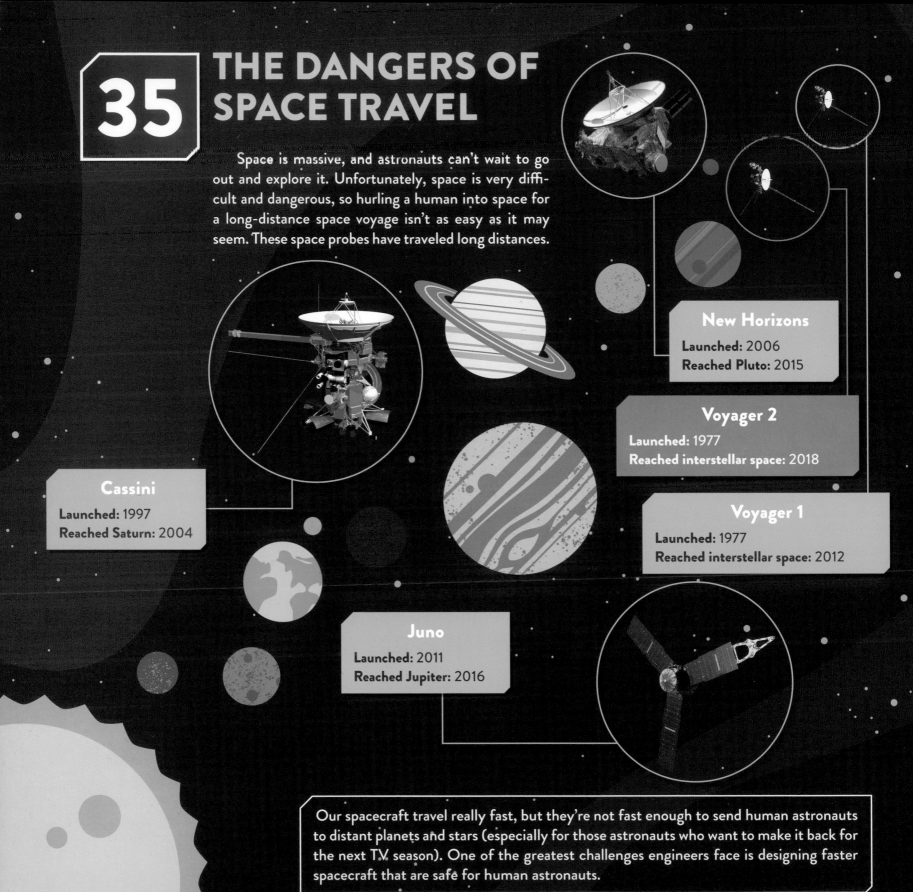

THE DANGERS OF SPACE TRAVEL

Space is massive, and astronauts can't wait to go out and explore it. Unfortunately, space is very difficult and dangerous, so hurling a human into space for a long-distance space voyage isn't as easy as it may seem. These space probes have traveled long distances.

New Horizons

Launched: 2006
Reached Pluto: 2015

Voyager 2

Launched: 1977
Reached interstellar space: 2018

Cassini

Launched: 1997
Reached Saturn: 2004

Voyager 1

Launched: 1977
Reached interstellar space: 2012

Juno

Launched: 2011
Reached Jupiter: 2016

Our spacecraft travel really fast, but they're not fast enough to send human astronauts to distant planets and stars (especially for those astronauts who want to make it back for the next TV season). One of the greatest challenges engineers face is designing faster spacecraft that are safe for human astronauts.

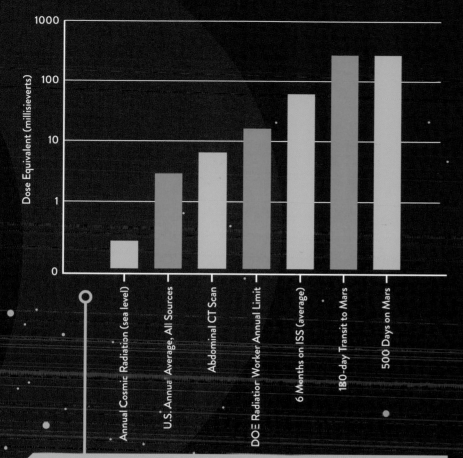

Dose Equivalent (millisieverts)

1000
100
10
1
0

- Annual Cosmic Radiation (sea level)
- U.S. Annual Average, All Sources
- Abdominal CT Scan
- DOE Radiation Worker Annual Limit
- 6 Months on ISS (average)
- 180-day Transit to Mars
- 500 Days on Mars

Bacteria in spacecraft can develop mutations that can make them more dangerous to humans. One study showed that a single bacterium developed an average of 12 genetic mutations in space. One of these mutations allowed the bacteria to reproduce more easily.

Radiation exposure is a major concern to the health of astronauts. Excessive radiation exposure can cause astronauts to develop cancer, dementia, and other serious (and often life-threatening) health problems.

Our bones and muscles are designed to bear weight, and the weightlessness in space causes our bodies to get a little "mushy." Even on short space flights, astronauts experience muscle atrophy (loss of muscle mass). Osteoporosis, a serious form of bone loss, is a real concern for extended space travel. A NASA study found that the astronauts lost about 10% of the bone mass in their femurs (thigh bones) during a 6-month stay in space, and it took 3–4 years on Earth for their bodies to replenish this mass.

55

36 JOURNEY TO THE STARS! (BETTER PACK A LUNCH)

So far, we've been limited to space travel within (or in the case of Voyager, juuuust outside) our own solar system. But someday, scientists may find a way to send probes—or people—to other stars. The following are six proposed methods of how we might get there.

1

In the 1950s, NASA proposed Project Orion, a spacecraft powered by the explosions of nuclear bombs! Several versions of Orion were proposed, including one that could theoretically reach 3% of light speed and reach the nearest star to the solar system, Alpha Centauri, within 130 years.

2
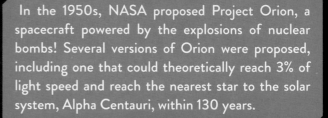
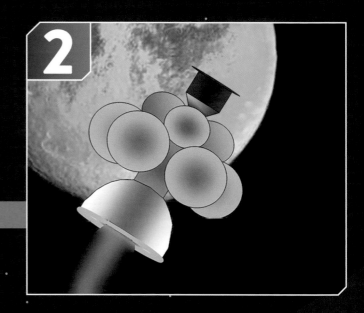

Project Daedalus was designed by British Interplanetary Society (BIS) engineers in the 1970s. The proposal called for a nuclear fusion engine to fire for nearly 4 years, pushing the probe up to 12% of light speed and to Barnard's Star (5.9 light-years away) in less than 50 years.

3

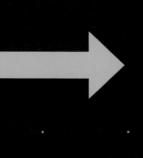

The Bussard ramjet, proposed by physicist Robert Bussard in 1960, is not a specific craft, but an idea for improving propulsion. To avoid needing huge fuel tanks, the ramjet would "scoop" hydrogen from surrounding space with an electromagnetic field to fuel its engine.

4

In 2009, the BIS began Project Icarus, an update of the Daedalus design with modern technologies. Although the project is still ongoing, improvements include using lasers to ignite the fusion reactions and designing a way to slow the craft after it reaches a target star.

5

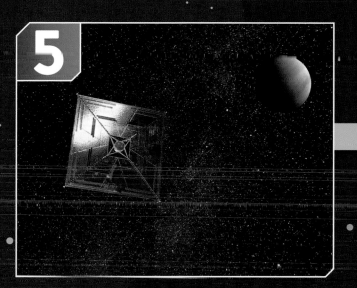

Light sails are proposed huge sheets of material unfurled by craft in space. Energy from light—the sun or powerful lasers—would hit one side of the sails, pushing the craft forward. The Breakthrough Starshot project plans to accelerate a fleet of light sail nanocraft up to 20% of light speed.

6

A magnetic sail would work much like a light sail, but would use a magnetic field, rather than electromagnetic energy, to "ride" the solar wind. Magnetic sails would resemble "space spiderwebs" of long superconducting wires around a spacecraft, used to create the magnetic field for propulsion.

Um . . . maybe I'll just wait for the next bus.

SPACE BUS

DON'T KNOCK IT IF IT'S NOT A ROCKET

So far, humans have relied on rockets to escape Earth's gravity and travel into space. But rockets are expensive, complicated, and sometimes dangerous. Ideally, we'd find ways into space that don't involve tons of exploding fuel—and below are six that have been proposed.

1 Elevators

Space elevators are proposed thin cables that would be very, very long—more than 22,000 miles high! Anchored to the ground, anything that could "shimmy" up the cable could be delivered right into space—but we don't know of a material that is strong enough to work.

2 Tethers

Space tethers would be long cables dangling from orbiting satellites that could "catch" payloads from planes or rockets at low altitudes, then pull them up higher into space. Rotating tethers, like skyhooks or rotavators, might even "catch and fling" craft upward as they spin.

3 Lasers

With the right spacecraft design, a powerful laser (or lasers) on the ground could fire at the craft, searing off part of a special surface. The exhaust created could push the craft forward at extremely high speeds, perhaps enough to make it into orbit.

4

Slingatron

Speaking of flinging (or slinging), the slingatron would spin craft in a spiral to build up enormous speed, then launch them up and out of the atmosphere. However, because of the g-forces this would generate, the slingatron likely couldn't be used to send manned craft into space.

5

Towers

NASA scientist and sci-fi author Geoffrey Landis has proposed building a tower 100 km (62 miles) high. Satellites or probes carried to the top would have an easier launch from high up, where gravity is weaker. A "space pier" composed of many such towers linked together is another idea.

6

Spaceplanes

Scientists are developing "spaceplanes" that they hope will be able to launch like a jet, travel high enough to escape gravity, and enter space, then later descend and land like a plane again on a runway. So far, planes can deliver satellites into low orbit, but not farther—yet.

You could always try clicking your heels three times. It worked for me.

THE SWISS ARMY KNIFE OF SPACE

When you have a hammer, everything looks like a nail. When you have a space station or an orbiting telescope, you need a special tool. NASA's pistol-grip tool (or PGT) fits the bill, designed specifically for space-based tinkering.

Torque and RPM can be programmed by astronauts—or remotely by mission control.

Like a cordless power drill, the PGT can tighten or loosen screws and other fasteners.

It withstands 500° F temperature shifts (from direct sunlight to darkness during spacewalks).

The oversized handle and triggers are designed for use with bulky spacesuit gloves.

It's no sonic screwdriver. But I guess it's pretty cool.

The tool of choice for astronauts servicing the ISS, Hubble Telescope, and more!

STICK THE LANDING

39

The Curiosity rover had one of the most harrowing landings in history, partially due to the signal delay between Earth and Mars. If something went seriously wrong after Curiosity entered Mars's atmosphere, NASA wouldn't even know about it until after Curiosity crashed to the ground.

7 MIN

Time it took Curiosity to land from atmosphere.

13 MIN 48 SECS

Time it took for a signal to reach Curiosity from Earth.

1 Deploy Parachute

- Slows speed of landing
- Parachute weighs 100 pounds (45 kg) but can withstand 65,000 pounds (29, 484 kg) of force

2 Activate Rockets

- Even with a parachute to slow down speed, the rover was moving too fast to make a safe landing
- Rockets allow for a gentle, controlled landing

3 Use Sky Crane

- If the rocket device directly landed the craft, it would kick up a lot of dust, which could severely damage the rover's instruments
- The sky crane and flyaway allowed the rover to land gently without kicking up excess dust and dirt

40 TIPPING OUR HATS TO CITIZEN SCIENTISTS

You don't need your own rocket ship or an infrared telescope to make an important space discovery. Some of the coolest space discoveries have been made by normal, everyday science buffs (just like you!) who volunteer their time to help astronomers collect or review data. Here are some of the recent discoveries by citizen scientists.

In 2017, citizen scientists discovered that the sun has a fairly close little buddy—a brown dwarf star about 100 light-years away.

In 2012, using data from the Spitzer Space Telescope, volunteers from the online Milky Way Project discovered 5,000 space bubbles. Space bubbles are caused by the formation of new stars. These citizen scientists discovered about 10 times more bubbles than previous projects had.

In 2012, Yale University's citizen scientist group, Planet Hunters, discovered an exoplanet in a four-star system, Kepler-64b. This planet was called PH1 for Planet Hunters 1.

An Aurora Named Steve sounds like a goofy comedy movie, but it was an actual discovery by citizen scientists. Northern lights gazers took pictures of an unusual streak of light that appeared in the sky. They posted the pics to social media and nicknamed the streak "Steve" (after the hedge in the animated movie *Over the Hedge*). Scientists are using satellite data to determine the cause of "Steve," but they believe it is a common phenomenon that simply hasn't been captured before now.

BIBLIOGRAPHY

EarthSky
http://earthsky.org

European Space Agency
http://www.esa.int

NASA
https://www.nasa.gov

NASA Goddard Space Flight Center: Imagine the Universe!
https://imagine.gsfc.nasa.gov

NASA Solar System Exploration
https://solarsystem.nasa.gov

NASA Space Place
https://spaceplace.nasa.gov

Sky & Telescope
http://skyandtelescope.com

Smithsonian.com
http://www.smithsonianmag.com

Space.com
https://www.space.com

Universe Today
https://www.universetoday.com

ABOUT THE AUTHORS

Jenn and Charlie are Boston-based science nerds who met through stand-up comedy. By day, Jenn writes science textbooks and Charlie slings data for a cancer research company. By night, they make comedy films and debate whether quarter moons are half light or half dark.

Jenn Dlugos

Charlie Hatton

IMAGE CREDITS

The publisher would like to thank the following for their permission to reproduce their illustrations:

Abbreviation key: t-top; m-middle; b-bottom; l-left; r-right

GARDEN BIRDS
OF NORTH AMERICA

GARDEN BIRDS
OF NORTH AMERICA

SCOTT WEIDENSAUL

GALLERY BOOKS

A QUINTET BOOK
produced for
GALLERY BOOKS
An imprint of W. H. Smith Publishers Inc.
112 Madison Avenue
New York, New York 10016

ISBN 0-8317-3753-0

This book was designed and produced by
Quintet Publishing Limited
6 Blundell Street
London N7 9BH

Creative Director: Peter Bridgewater
Art Director: Ian Hunt
Designer: Stuart Walden
Editor: Shaun Barrington

Typeset in Great Britain by
Central Southern Typesetters, Eastbourne
Manufactured in Hong Kong by
Regent Publishing Services Limited
Printed in Hong Kong by
Leefung-Asco Printers Limited

CONTENTS

INTRODUCTION

Nut bags, which can be hung almost anywhere, are suitable for finches and chickadees.

Purpose-built metal or plastic nut and scrap baskets should not have sharp edges or points which could damage birds' legs.

Once the chickadees have eaten the coconut, the empty shell can be filled with "bird cake," a mixture of seeds, dried fruit and kitchen scraps, bound with suet, lard or dripping.

*B*y most counts, there are more than 800 species of birds that breed on the North American continent, or drop in from abroad on a regular basis. It is an amazing number, representing an equally amazing variety – from tiny hummingbirds to the endangered California condor, with its 10-foot wingspan, from brilliantly colored warblers through waterfowl, herons, woodpeckers and owls.

Many of these birds live in inaccessible locations – on the high slopes of mountains, the arctic tundra, in swamps and wilderness areas. But many of them make their homes near ours, in backyards and shade trees. Some breed there, some visit only in the winter, others pass through during migration. For lack of a better term, they are "garden birds," those species most likely to be seen by the average person.

This book is an introduction to 80 of those birds. It is by no means a complete list, but is meant to give an overview of the species that are most widespread, and most likely to be met with close to home. Each bird's life history is briefly discussed, in the hope of engendering a greater appreciation for the role each plays in the environment, for their beauty and for the vibrancy they bring to the outdoors.

OPPOSITE The large seed cracking bill of the gorgeous northern cardinal indicates its preference for seeds, fruits and small nuts (see page 73).
ABOVE Another bird which can easily be tempted to the feeder – but is not perhaps quite so welcome – is the more aggressive and opportunistic common grackle (see page 86).

ABOVE The familiar robin is comfortable around people, and is particularly attracted by certain plants and most fruit trees: honeysuckle, bittersweet, sumac – and a real favorite is cherry (see page 50).

A nut feeder and drinking cup combined; remember not to place the feeder too far away from protective cover.

Birds are more popular with the general public than ever before. Millions of people tote binoculars everywhere they go, some traveling the world to add new species to their "life list" of birds. Millions more have a hard time telling one kind from the other, but spread a bounty of seeds for the birds each winter at their feeders, enjoying the excitement of having wildlife so close at hand. Beginner or expert, all realize that birds add an immeasurable amount of joy to the world.

Attracting birds to your yard is easy, and while this book is not meant to be a how-to guide, there are some basic principles that should be mentioned. Most birds feel more comfortable if there is cover close by — trees, shrubs, thickets, hedges, somewhere they can escape to if danger should threaten. Many first-time bird feeders place the feeding station too far from protective cover, then wonder why the birds stay away.

Food can be provided in two ways: as a regular handout, such as at a feeder, or by planting specific sorts of flowers, shrubs and trees. The plantings must be geared for the sort of bird one wishes to attract, because tastes differ; hummingbirds sip flower nectar,

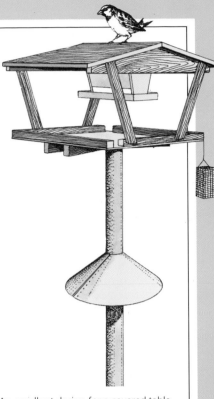

and are drawn by red, tubular flowers like trumpet creeper, while cedar waxwings prefer berries and fruit, making mountain ash a perfect choice.

Feeders come in a bewildering array of sizes and styles. The best are often the simplest – a covered tray, set on a pole about five feet tall near a tree or bushes. For smaller birds like chickadees and titmice, plastic tube feeders work well.

There are also many kinds of food on the market. As a matter of course, avoid commercial bird seedmixes, which contain large quantities of junk seeds, like rape and milo, that few birds eat. By far, the best overall food is sunflower seed – specifically, oil sunflower, a small hulled, black variety that contains less waste and higher nourishment than standard striped seeds. For ground-feeders like doves, cracked corn and white proso millet are tops. For best economy, buy seed directly from a feed mill, if possible.

Beef suet, available from the meat counter of most super-markets, is a terrific cold-weather food for chickadees, titmice,

An excellent design for a covered table including drainage at the corners of the base plate and a metal cone to thwart cat and squirrel raiding parties.

ABOVE Water should be made available during nesting and the winter months for the song sparrow (see page 78); it will nest in any brushy area, on or close to the ground – including city parks and gardens.

9

Wrens will nest in a variety of objects including flowerpots, coconuts and pipes, but can also build their own nests.

nuthatches and woodpeckers. Suspend the suet from a tree branch in a plastic mesh onion bag, or put it in a commercial suet feeder. Peanut butter, rolled oats, fat and corn meal, heated and mixed thoroughly, makes a very good winter food, chilled and cut into cakes.

Some birds like specialty foods: titmice and blue jays enjoy peanut kernels, and goldfinches go absolutely crazy over niger seed, commonly sold as "thistle." Such seed is hideously expensive, however, and goldfinches do just as well with oil sunflower seed.

Don't overlook the value of water in attracting birds. A bird-bath, cleaned and filled regularly to reduce the chance of disease, will be a magnet during warm weather — but only if it, like the feeders, has ample cover nearby. During the spring and fall migration, warblers, orioles and thrushes — indeed, most song-birds — can be lured from hiding by the sound of dripping water. A hose, hung from a low branch and just barely trickling into a dish below, can do the trick.

ABOVE The typical ground nest of the western meadowlark, with its arching roof (see page 83). Both the eastern and western meadowlark are birds of the grasslands and prairies.

ABOVE Tree swallows (see page 33) cannot make their own nest cavities and must rely upon woodpeckers and tree diseases; not surprisingly therefore, a nest box is the best way to attract them to your yard.

Even if your bird-watching is confined to a glance out the kitchen window every now and then, a pair of binoculars and a good field guide will add greatly to your enjoyment. The best all-around binoculars are 7-by-35s; that is, they magnify objects seven times (the 35 refers to the width of the lens).

There are many field guides on the market, but three are excellent for beginners: Roger Tory Peterson's venerable A Field Guide to the Birds *(Houghton Mifflin) comes in an eastern and western edition, and is perhaps the most widely used.* Birds of North America, *by Robbins, Brun and Zim (Golden Press), covers all of the continent's birds in one compact volume.* Field Guide to Birds of North America, *published by the National Geographic Society, is more detailed than the other two, including illustrations of many subspecies, but that feature may actually be a confusing drawback to the neophyte.*

The sight of a small, colorful bird awakens something within everyone, and can lead to a lifetime of fascination. It can also lead to a greater awareness of the fragility of our environment, and an intense commitment to preserve its threatened treasures — quite an accomplishment for so tiny a creature.

This kind of box, with the entrance at the side, will attract creepers.

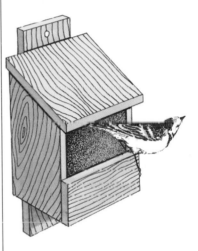

Open-fronted boxes like this are ideal for species like the robin and the phoebe.

Using a leather strap to secure a box will avoid damaging the tree.

FROM HAWK

TO HUMMINGBIRD

A Species Directory of Garden Birds

OPPOSITE *Mimus polyglottos,* the northern mocking bird, best known for its endless medley of other birds' songs (see page 52).

SHARP-SHINNED HAWK
ACCIPITER STRIATUS

Little larger than a mourning dove, the sharp-shinned hawk makes up in daring and bravado what it lacks in size. Found from the arctic treeline south through almost every wooded habitat in North America, the "sharpie" is also the raptor most likely to be seen in suburbia – especially in winter, when hunger prompts many to stalk bird feeders for sparrows and finches.

Like most birds of prey, female sharp-shinned hawks are about a third larger than their mates, possibly an adaptation that allows a pair to hunt for prey of differing sizes. Adults sport a slate-gray head and back, with rusty barring on the belly and bright red eyes. Most sharpies seen at feeders, however, are inexperienced, yellow-eyed immature birds, which are brown above, with a white, streaked breast.

Regardless of age or plumage, sharp-shinned hawks have the classic form of the accipiters, or forest hawks – a long tail for easy maneuvering, and short, rounded wings that provide rapid bursts of speed. Sharp-shinneds are primarily songbird hunters, relying on surprise and a frantic dash to bring down their prey.

DISTRIBUTION AND IDENTIFICATION

PLUMAGE Adult: gray head and back, with rusty bars on belly; long tail and short, rounded wings. Immatures: brown above, with white, streaked breast.

HABITAT Wooded areas.

FOOD Birds (sparrows, finches, etc.) and mice.

NEST Simple, built of sticks; usually in conifers such as pine.

EGGS 4–5 eggs; white with brown blotches.

Spring finds the sharp-shinneds in their northern breeding grounds. This species almost always picks a conifer as its nest tree – usually a pine with lots of concealing branches, growing in a dense stand. The nest itself is a rather straightforward affair built of sticks, into which four or five eggs are laid. The newly hatched chicks are blind, almost naked and completely helpless – "atricial" is the actual ornithological term. At first, the adults must snip off tiny pieces of meat for their young, but within a few weeks the babies – now cloaked in down and sprouting flight feathers – can themselves rip apart the birds and mice brought to the nest.

A closely related species, the Cooper's hawk, is slightly larger than the sharpie but so close in appearance that even experienced birders have trouble telling the two apart.

AMERICAN KESTREL
FALCO SPARVERIUS

Light as air, a kestrel hovers in a summer's breeze, flapping its wings to a blur. Below, a meadow vole moves in the grass – a tiny movement, but enough for the hawk's sharp eyes to notice. Wings folded and its taloned feet extended, the kestrel drops, pinning the small rodent to the ground.

The American kestrel is perhaps the most common – and certainly the most visible – of the continent's birds of prey. Although also found in forest meadows and marshes, the kestrel (formerly known as the sparrow hawk) is first and foremost a bird of the open countryside, where it is often seen sitting on telephone wires and dead trees.

It is also the smallest hawk, a robin-sized raptor with long, tapered wings and streamlined tail – attributes it shares with its relative, the peregrine falcon. Unlike most hawks, male and female kestrels are colored differently. The male has bluish-gray wings and a bright, rusty-orange tail, both of which in the female are a duller orange, barred with black. Both sexes have black "mustache" marks on the sides of their faces, and caps of blue and orange – all in all, a handsome combination.

Kestrels hunt from either the wing or a perch. Their habit of hovering 40 or 50 feet in the air earned

DISTRIBUTION AND IDENTIFICATION

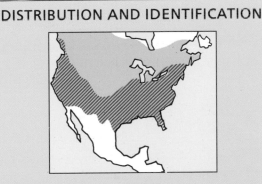

PLUMAGE Male: bluish-gray wings, orange tail. Female: dull orange tail and wings. Both have black "mustaches" on sides of face, blue and orange caps; long, tapered wings and streamlined tails.
HABITAT Open countryside, also meadows and marshes.
FOOD Small mammals, especially meadow voles; songbirds; insects in summer.
NEST In hollow trees; will accept artificial birdboxes.
EGGS 4–5 eggs; white or tan with fine brown speckling.

them the name windhover in many rural areas, where they search for small mammals and songbirds. During the summer, insects – especially grasshoppers – are an important food supply as well, but by far the biggest menu item, regardless of the season, is the meadow vole, a small, mouse-like rodent.

Far more than most hawks, kestrels seem at ease around people. In the wild they nest in hollow trees, but because dead trees with the right sized holes are rare, they readily accept artificial nest boxes. Built in the same general shape as a bluebird box, a kestrel box should be about 15 inches deep, with a three-inch entrance hole. The box should be placed in the open, on a utility pole, the side of a barn, a tall tree or a pole erected for the purpose.

NORTHERN BOBWHITE
COLINUS VIRGINIANUS

That clear, two-noted call "Bob-whiiiite." "Bob-whiiiite!" rings out each morning in spring across much of the South and Midwest, as coveys of bobwhite awake and the males begin to seek mates.

Plump and round, a bobwhite is only about 10 inches long, including the short tail. When a covey (as quail flocks are called) explodes into flight, the startled observer sees only whirring wings and brown bodies hurtling in every direction. In quieter moments, though, one can see the russet, black and white feather pattern that camouflages the bobwhite, and the bold black-and-white facial markings of the male. Females are patterned similarly, but have brownish faces instead of white.

Although they range into New York and west to Wyoming, the bobwhite's stronghold is the South, where they inhabit weedy fields adjacent to fence-rows or brushy forests. In many areas, they are common as well in residential areas (provided the developers have left some vestiges of unmanicured habitat among the lawns and swimming pools). Their staple diet is weed seeds, grain, corn, sprouts and some nuts, supplemented with insects.

The female bobwhite picks a hollow in dense grass for her nest, little more than a shallow bowl of woven grass and weeds with an arch of woven blades to hide it from above. The eggs – 15, on average – are incubated by both the male and female, and hatch in about three weeks. Almost as soon as their down dries, the chicks are able to walk and feed themselves – a far cry from the helpless young of songbirds. The parents' duty is primarily to guard the young. Should a predator be seen, the adults give a rapid alarm cry, which the chicks react to instinctively, scattering for cover and staying motionless until the all-clear is sounded; should a dog, fox or person come too close, the adult may try to lure it away with a very convincing broken-wing imitation.

DISTRIBUTION AND IDENTIFICATION

PLUMAGE Russet, black and white pattern; short tail. Male: black-and-white face markings; female has brownish face.

HABITAT Weedy fields near forests, fencerows; also, residential areas.

FOOD Weed seeds, grain, corn, sprouts, nuts; also insects.

NEST Shallow bowl of woven grass and weeds, with arch of woven blades; in hollow and dense grass.

EGGS 10–20 eggs; white.

BAND-TAILED PIGEON
COLUMBA FASCIATA

The largest wild dove in North America, the band-tailed pigeon occupies two distinct sections of the West – the Pacific coast from British Columbia to Baja California and through central California; and in a large area including parts of Colorado, New Mexico, Utah, Arizona and Texas, where populations are smaller.

Along the coast, the band-tail is a resident of oak forests, which provide both nesting sites and abundant acorns, its favorite food, while the interior population lives in pine forests. Band-tails are at ease feeding in trees, something few doves do, and they can be quite acrobatic as they maneuver their relatively heavy bodies among thin oak branches.

In shape, band-tailed pigeons closely resemble feral rock doves, the common pigeon of cities. But, as the name suggests, the band-tail has a broad, gray band across the tip of its tail, and a narrow white crescent on the nape of the neck; it is also somewhat larger, at 14 or 15 inches, than the rock dove. The sexes are basically alike, with a purplish-blue breast (brighter in males), a black-tipped, yellow beak, and yellow feet.

During the breeding season, band-tailed pigeons are fairly secretive. The nest is a crude platform of twigs, built close to the tree trunk, and may be part of a loose colony of pigeon nests. The band-tail usually lays only one egg in each brood, but may nest up to three times a year.

In the winter, members of the coastal population band together in flocks that sometimes reach the thousands. The interior population, and birds from the northern coast, are migratory.

DISTRIBUTION AND IDENTIFICATION

PLUMAGE Purplish-blue breast, broad gray band across tip of tail; narrow white crescent on nape of neck.

HABITAT Oak and pine forests.

FOOD Primarily acorns, also other nuts, berries and fruits.

NEST Crude platform of twigs built close to tree trunk.

EGGS 1 egg; pure white.

MOURNING DOVE
ZENAIDA MACROURA

It seems likely that, in the days predating European settlement in North America, the mourning dove was something of a bit player in the continent's aviafauna, restricted to open river valleys and natural meadows. The mighty, unbroken forests belonged to its close relative, the passenger pigeon, which moved in flocks numbering in the billions.

Times certainly have changed. The forests have been fragmented by a patchwork of fields and towns. The passenger pigeon, unable to cope with the dual threat of unrestricted hunting and habitat destruction, is extinct. And the mourning dove is now one of the most common birds in North America – and becoming even more common each year.

The reason is that man has created the very conditions a mourning dove needs to thrive – an abundance of grain fields and weedy patches, ponds and streams for water, pine thickets for nighttime roosting, not to mention bird feeders to tide the doves over winter's hardships. Couple that with the dove's prodigious reproductive rate, and it's little wonder that their plaintive call can be heard in virtually every corner of the United States and southern Canada.

Roughly a foot long, mourning doves are brownish, with a pink cast to the head and breast.

They are lovely in a simple sort of way, lacking the flash of many songbirds; the only flashy thing about them is their pointed tail, edged with white. Males differ from females only in having a patch of pink iridescence on the neck.

Doves are confirmed seed eaters, gleaning waste grain from harvested fields, and picking the seeds of weeds like fox-tail grass. In the winter, cracked corn lures them to feeding stations, although they usually avoid raised feeders, preferring to stay on the ground.

DISTRIBUTION AND IDENTIFICATION

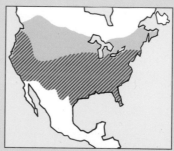

PLUMAGE Brownish, with pink cast to head and breast; pointed tail edged with white. Male has patch of pink iridescence on neck.

HABITAT Grain fields, weedy patches, pine thickets.

FOOD Seeds and insects.

NEST Shaky platform of twigs in tree or shrub.

EGGS 2–3 eggs; plain white.

YELLOW-BILLED CUCKOO
COCCYZUS AMERICANUS

If ever there was a true "ugly duckling" tale in the bird world, it would be that of the yellow-billed cuckoo. The newly hatched young are, in the words of one early naturalist, "repulsive, black, greasy looking creatures . . . the sprouting quills only add to their general ugliness." When threatened, they hiss like a snake. Yet within two weeks, the porcupine-like feather quills erupt into a soft cloak – a pure white breast, brown back, burnt sienna wings and eventually a tail nearly as long as the bird's body, edged in black and white. The final result is as dapper a bird as lives in North America.

Unlike the European cuckoo, which lays its eggs in the nests of other birds, the yellow-billed cuckoo (and its cousin, the black-billed cuckoo) generally cares for its own young. Both are residents of woodlands, thickets and orchards, nesting in low trees and shrubs. The rapid-fire *kuk-kuk-kuk-kowlp-kowlp-kowlp* of the yellow-billed is a common summer sound in all but the northwest corner of the U.S., and seems to be especially noticeable before thunderstorms, earning the bird the name "rain crow" in some regions.

Insects are a cuckoo's food, especially large, hairy caterpillars ordinarily shunned by other birds. Such a rough, spiny diet would disagree with most birds, but the cuckoo's digestive system seems to take the caterpillar hair in its stride.

Courtship takes places shortly after the cuckoos return to their breeding grounds. The male may offer tidbits to his potential mate – perhaps a squirming tent caterpillar, or a large beetle. Her reaction is that of a young chick: crouched, her wings quivering, she gapes and accepts the food. The nest is a haphazard mess of twigs scarcely deep enough to hold the eggs, usually built in a low bush or shrubby tree close to the ground.

DISTRIBUTION AND IDENTIFICATION

PLUMAGE Pure white breast, brown back, burnt sienna wings; long tail edged in black and white.

HABITAT Woodlands, thickets, orchards.

FOOD Insect, especially caterpillars.

NEST Haphazard mess of twigs built in low trees, shrubs and bushes.

EGGS 3–4 pale blue-green eggs.

EASTERN SCREECH-OWL
OTUS ASIO

As dusk falls in the woodlot, a quavering wail splits the air. A moment later it is repeated, starting high but descending rapidly, a tremulous call like the whinny of a horse. The screech-owl is up and about again.

At about eight inches, the screech-owl is commonly mistaken for a "baby" owl – and it does look like a miniature version of the much larger great horned owl, with the same mottled plumage and erect ear tufts. The tufts are nothing more than feather clumps, and rather than having anything to do with hearing (the actual ears are holes in the side of the skull), serve as a form of camouflage. A screech-owl, sitting tight against the weathered trunk of a tree, has only to close its bright yellow eyes in order to disappear into the scenery. There are two color phases, gray and brick-orange, that are not linked to sex or age.

A small bundle of fluff, the eastern screech-owl is nonetheless an efficient predator, hunting for mice,

insects, small birds, frogs and lizards. For nighttime navigation and silent flight, it has large, forward-facing eyes that gather faint light, fluffy edges on the major wing feathers to deaden sound, and eight needle-sharp talons.

Screech-owls have adapted quite well to people, and are probably the most common bird of prey around human habitation. All they require are old trees with holes, for hiding and for nesting. A large birdbox, with at least a three-inch opening and placed on the trunk of a tree in a wooded part of your property, may attract these owls, both as a nest site or as winter roost. In return, the lucky homeowner will get free concerts of wild owlish music – certainly a fair trade.

DISTRIBUTION AND IDENTIFICATION

PLUMAGE Mottled; erect ear tufts (feather clumps). Two color phases: gray and brick-orange.

HABITAT Wooded areas, both rural and residential.

FOOD Mice, insects, small birds, frogs and lizards.

NEST Old trees with holes; takes to birdboxes.

EGGS 4 or 5 eggs; pure white.

COMMON NIGHTHAWK
CHORDEILES MINOR

No raptor at all, the nighthawk is an insect eater that "hawks" its food in swooping flight – hence the misleading name. Once restricted to old forest-fire burns and rocky river beds, the nighthawk has also taken well to the flat, graveled roofs of city buildings, making it a common sight at dusk in summer.

As its name suggests, the nighthawk is nocturnal, heading aloft just as sunset fades to twilight. It shares the sky with bats, but unlike them has no radar to track down the moths and beetles on which it feeds, apparently relying on vision to pick out the tiny forms of bugs against the dim sky. As it flies it calls, a regular, almost mechanical *peent* that many city-dwellers mistake for a machine.

Found from southern Canada south into Mexico, the nighthawk can easily be identified by its extremely long, tapered wings, each marked with a bold white slash. Its plumage is a grizzled mix of gray, black and white that helps it blend in with rocks and pebbles. The bird's feet are tiny, and are almost useless for walking – something it rarely does, in any event.

To impress his mate, the male nighthawk executes a series of spectacular looping dives, punctuated with *peents*. As the flying bird bottoms out and begins his upward climb, air rushing over his vibrating wing feathers makes a pronounced booming sound.

The nighthawk does not make even a pretense of a nest, simply laying its two eggs directly on the ground. Should the "nest" site be a building roof, the temperature on a hot summer day will quickly climb to levels lethal to the unhatched embryos, but the female will not budge, shading the eggs through the long hours, fluttering her throat to dissipate excess body heat. On one rooftop, the surface temperature was measured at a brutal 142 degrees, but researchers found that a female nighthawk was able to keep her eggs a relatively cool 115 degrees.

DISTRIBUTION AND IDENTIFICATION

PLUMAGE Mixture of gray, black and white, with bold white slashes on long, tapered wings.

HABITAT Rocky river beds, forest-fire burns; also city buildings.

FOOD Insects.

NEST Eggs laid directly on ground or rooftop.

EGGS 2 eggs; heavily spotted with gray-brown.

CHIMNEY SWIFT
CHAETURA PELAGICA

Even more so than the nighthawk, civilization has been kind to the chimney swift – so kind, in fact, that it is rarely seen nesting in hollow trees, once its traditional habitat. Instead, chimney swifts have adopted the smokestacks, ventilation shafts and chimneys of North America's cities, where its unique "flying cigar" shape is a common sight overhead.

A swift is small – about five inches – and an appropriately sooty shade of brown. Its wings are outlandishly long in relation to its body size, a pair of feathered scimitars that give the bird quite phenomenal speed. The tail is short, and the stiff central quills of each tail feather extend beyond the tip for a short distance, where they act as a brace when the bird is clinging upright inside a chimney. Its legs are short and almost incapable of walking, but the feet of a swift are strongly clawed, much like a woodpecker's, for gripping rough stone or wood surfaces.

A swift's nest is a marvel, constructed of twigs that are glued, with the bird's sticky saliva, to the inside surface of the chimney. The nest is just barely big enough to hold the four or five eggs, but once the chicks hatch and begin to grow, they use their claws to scramble out, clinging tightly to the brick or rock wall nearby.

DISTRIBUTION AND IDENTIFICATION

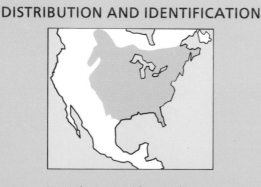

PLUMAGE Sooty brown, with very long wings and short tail.

HABITAT Chimneys, smokestacks and ventilation shafts.

FOOD Flying insects.

NEST Twigs stuck together with bird's saliva, built inside of chimney, smokestack, silo, etc.

EGGS 4 or 5 eggs; plain white.

A chimney that attracts one pair of swifts is likely to attract many, because this is a highly social species – especially as summer wanes. By August, the swifts begin to flock, feeding feverishly to lay on fat reserves. At night, they gather in huge communal roosts of up to several thousand, swirling around above the chosen chimney or silo in a seething, gray mass, twittering up a storm, then spiraling down into the opening. From a distance, the effect is startling, resembling a smoke cloud reversing itself to flow down, rather than up.

RUBY-THROATED HUMMINGBIRD
ARCHILOCHUS COLUBRIS

Flitting from blossom to blossom like a bee – and only a little bigger – the ruby-throated humming-bird is the crown jewel of Eastern gardens, a shining wonder of iridescent green and red shimmering in the sunlight.

Hummingbirds are so small that it is difficult to believe they really are birds (and some early settlers, in fact, thought them more akin to insects). The ruby-throat – the only species in eastern North America – is three and a half inches long, about average as hummers go. Nearly a quarter of that length is taken up by its long, rapier bill, which hides an even longer tongue for sipping flower nectar.

Courtship includes a display flight by the male that resembles the swinging of a pendulum, after which the female (identified by her white throat) begins to build the nest. She uses plant down, securing it to the top of a small branch with spider silk, building the nest layer by layer until she forms a tiny cup. As a last step, she will shingle the outside with small bits of lichen, effectively camouflaging it from casual notice.

The eggs she lays are no larger than peas, and are incubated for about two weeks. It is alarming to watch a hummingbird feed her young, for she plunges her long beak almost completely down the chick's gullet before regurgitating the meal of nectar and small insects.

The most remarkable thing about any humming-bird, however, is its flight. A ruby-throat can beat its stiff wings at an amazing 50 times a second, moving forward, backward and even hovering in place to feed. Its metabolic rate is equally ferocious, with its heart beating up to 1,200 times per minute.

All hummingbirds, including the ruby-throat, have an attraction for red or orange flowers – a fact that nature-conscious gardeners play upon to attract them. Hummingbird favorites include monarda, trumpet creeper, red forms of salvia and nictotiana, pink or red impatiens and the cardinal flower.

Ruby-throated hummingbirds are not picky about their habitat, although they are most often found in woodland clearings where flowers are abundant.

DISTRIBUTION AND IDENTIFICATION

PLUMAGE Iridescent green above and white below. Male, red throat; female, white throat.

HABITAT Woodland clearings full of flowers; also suburban gardens.

FOOD Nectar of red and orange flowers, such as trumpet creeper, impatiens; small insects.

NEST Plant down, secured to a tree branch with spider silk; a tiny cup comprising layers and camou-flaged with bits of lichen.

EGGS 2 plain white eggs.

BLACK-CHINNED HUMMINGBIRD
ARCHILOCHUS ALEXANDRI

The American West is rich in hummingbirds, especially in the canyons of the Southwest. Some species have very limited ranges, but the black-chinned hummingbird is one of the most widespread, found from southern British Columbia and the Pacific coast, east to Texas.

DISTRIBUTION AND IDENTIFICATION

PLUMAGE Iridescent green above and white below. Male, black gorget, with purple patch at bottom; female has white throat.

HABITAT Meadows, fields and mountain slopes.

FOOD Nectar, flying insects.

NEST Built in branches of trees and vines, like ruby-throated's but for lichen camouflage.

EGGS 2 eggs; plain white.

Female black-chinneds are so similar to female ruby-throated hummingbirds that, where their ranges overlap in Texas, it is almost impossible to tell the two apart. Black-chinned males, however, sport a trademark black gorget, with a vibrant purple patch along the lower edge that shows up only in good light.

When the hillside meadows erupt with wildflowers in summer, this species can be found feeding on the nectar of Indian paintbrush and other blossoms, as well as snatching flying insects out of the air. Black-chinneds frequently follow the advance of warm weather up the slopes of the Rocky Mountains, moving to ever-higher altitudes as new fields of flowers open.

Nesting and care of the young are very like that of the ruby-throated hummingbird, its near relative. The nest is generally built in the branches of a tree or vine, and lacks the lichen shingling of a ruby-throat's. When they leave the nest the chicks resemble their mother, although in late summer the immature males will start to show a few flecks of black or purple on the throat. By the time they return from their wintering grounds in Mexico, they will have molted in a complete gorget, and will be ready to stake out a breeding territory for the coming summer.

NORTHERN FLICKER
COLAPTES AURATUS

With its colorful wing linings and rolling, *wick-wick-wick-wick-wick* call, the northern flicker is one of the best-known birds in North America, common from suburban lawns to deserts and northern forests.

The flicker is a woodpecker with a penchant for feeding on the ground, where it hunts for ants, its favorite food. About a foot long, its brown back is barred with black, and it flashes a large, white rump patch in flight. Depending on the part of the country, the wing linings may be bright yellow (in the East) or pinkish orange (in the West); the two color phases were once considered separate species. The sexes are similar, but males have mustache marks alongside the face that females lack – red in the western form, and black in the eastern.

In some areas, flickers were known as "high-holers" for their habit of chopping their nest cavity into a tree or utility pole 50 or 60 feet above the ground, although they will nest much closer to earth if locations are scarce. During the breeding season flickers can be highly territorial, chasing away others of their species with a sharp *wik-up, wik-up, wik-up* alarm call. If the intruder doesn't leave quickly enough, it might find itself bowled over by the outraged defender.

Unfortunately, flickers are no match for starlings, which will take over the nest hole that a pair of flickers spent a week or more patiently excavating. Bird-watchers have found that special nest boxes, as much as two feet deep and packed with sawdust, attract flickers but not starlings (who, obviously, have no need of human intervention), thus giving a helping hand to this beautiful bird.

DISTRIBUTION AND IDENTIFICATION

PLUMAGE Brown back barred with black; white rump in flight. Yellow wing linings in East, pinkish-orange in West. Eastern male, black "mustache" on face; western male, red "mustache".

HABITAT From suburbia to deserts and forests.

FOOD Ants and wood-boring insects.

NEST Cavity chopped into trees or utility poles, usually 50–60 ft above ground; will take to nest boxes 2 ft deep, packed with sawdust.

EGGS 6 or 7 eggs; glossy white.

RED-HEADED WOODPECKER
MELANERPES ERYTHOCEPHALUS

Absolutely unmistakable, the adult red-headed woodpecker certainly lives up to its name. From the neck up, its head is flaming scarlet, the only woodpecker with such a blazing field mark. In flight, this species cuts a striking figure, with a white rump, wing patches and breast set off by satiny black.

Although found from the Rockies east, red-headed woodpeckers have declined in the Northeast, where starlings compete aggressively for nest holes. In the South it is a much more common sight, hammering on dead trees for beetles or foraging for berries, ripening fruit and nuts. The red-head is not above taking the chicks of other songbirds, although such attacks are generally rare, and insects comprise the largest part of its diet.

Red-headed woodpeckers stick to fairly open country, like pastures, forest edges and parks, where the trees grow in widely spaced groves. The nest is chiseled into a tree or dead snag up to 80 feet above the ground. The immature birds have a brownish head with just a tinge of red to it, and lack also the glossy black back of the adult. By fall, however, the young begin to molt their juvenile plumage, and by the following May are in full adult color.

Red-headed woodpeckers are one of the few species of birds known to store food. In late summer,

DISTRIBUTION AND IDENTIFICATION

PLUMAGE Flaming scarlet head, pure white breast; jet black back with white rump and wing patches. Immatures, brownish head with tinge of red.

HABITAT Open country (pastures, parks, etc.) with trees in widely spaced groves.

FOOD Mostly insects, but also berries, seeds, fruit and nuts (stored for winter).

NEST Chiseled into tree or dead snag up to 80 ft above ground.

EGGS 4 or 5 eggs; pure white.

the woodpecker begins to gather acorns, nuts and seeds, stashing them away in knotholes and other natural cavities. Come winter, it will defend from other woodpeckers a territory encompassing these caches and a snug roost hole.

DOWNY WOODPECKER
PICOIDES PUBESCENS

A favorite of those who feed birds during the winter, the downy woodpecker is the most common member of its family, found in all but the desert and high arctic. As animated as a wind-up toy, its presence at a backyard feeder enlivens the dreariness of a cold, snowy day.

At less than seven inches, the downy is the smallest North American woodpecker. Both sexes have basically the same black-and-white pattern, but the male has a small patch of scarlet on the back of the head that the female lacks. Black spots on the downy's white outer tail feathers distinguish it from the almost identical hairy woodpecker, a slightly larger (and less common) species that shares its range.

Usually, the first clue that a downy woodpecker is nearby comes in the form of a soft, irregular tapping, as the bird chips away at bark and soft wood in its hunt for insects. In the spring, the male advertises his presence with a very rapid hammering, which serves the same purpose as a robin's song – to warn away rivals and to lure a mate. Such drumming is common among woodpeckers, and experienced birders can usually guess the species by the speed and loudness of the sound.

All woodpeckers, including the downy, are adapted to chopping wood for the insects hidden inside. The beak is strong, and the base of the skull is padded to absorb the shock of impact. The tongue is long and barbed for skewering insects. The feet have strong claws for gripping bark, and the tail feathers are stiff, to act as a brace when the bird leans back to start hammering.

Downy woodpeckers will take sunflower seeds, peanut hearts and cracked corn at a feeder, but the best way to attract them is to hang beef suet in a mesh bag from a tree branch.

DISTRIBUTION AND IDENTIFICATION

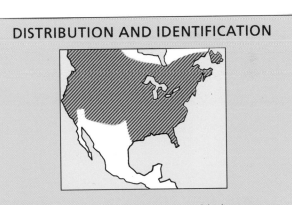

PLUMAGE Black and white pattern; black spots on white outer tail feathers. Male, small patch of red on back of head.

HABITAT Deciduous forests.

FOOD Insects; sunflower seeds, peanut hearts, cracked corn, beef suet at feeder.

NEST Excavates cavity in tree or stump, 20–50 ft above ground.

EGGS 4 or 5 eggs; pure white.

EASTERN KINGBIRD
TYRANNUS TYRANNUS

Heaven help the hawk that strays too close to a kingbird's nest. Out of the blue, the adults come racing in, dive-bombing the raptor while screaming their staccato, *dzeet-dzeet-dzeet-dzeet* call. The alarm often brings in other small birds, which mob the unfortunate hawk and chase it out of their territory. But usually the kingbird is the first to give chase, and the last to abandon the pursuit. After such a performance, the species' scientific name, *Tyrannus tyrannus*, seems appropriate.

The eastern kingbird is more widespread than its common name might indicate, ranging from the Canadian prairie provinces through the Great Plains and south to Florida. Wherever it lives, it is a conspicuous bird, flycatching from telephone wires or treetops, making hundreds of short, dashing flights a day to nab passing insects. Beekeepers have always disliked the kingbird, however, believing that it has a great taste for honeybees. Examination of stomach contents has shown that, while kingbirds do take some bees, they pose no great threat to hives.

There is no color difference between the sexes. Adults are white underneath with a black head and back. The black tail carries a white tip – a good field mark, and far better than the thin, red patch on the head, usually hidden by surrounding feathers.

The kingbird's nest is generally built near the end of tree branches, supported by a fork and woven out of weeds, grass and leaves. Kingbirds are not always terribly fussy about their nest site, however; they have been known to build in purple martin gourds, a rain gauge or an electric street light, and to take over the nest of a northern oriole.

DISTRIBUTION AND IDENTIFICATION

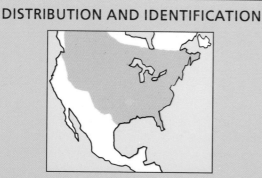

PLUMAGE Black head and back, white underneath. Thin red patch on head (often hidden). Black tail with white tip.
HABITAT Open areas, from prairies and farmland, to parks.
FOOD Insects (including bees).
NEST Woven from weeds, grasses and leaves; built near end of tree branches, supported by a fork; sometimes nest in drainpipes, street lights, purple martin gourds.
EGGS 3–5 eggs with heavy brown blotches.

WESTERN KINGBIRD
TYRANNUS VERTICALIS

In the ranchlands and fields of the West, around towns and wherever a fence provides a perch, the western kingbird makes its home. Like the eastern kingbird, it tirelessly harasses Swainson's hawks and other raptors that enter its territory, but unlike its eastern relative, the western kingbird is a degree more social, sometimes nesting in the same tree as another pair. Still others are wholly intolerant of neighbors – suggesting that birds, like people, are individuals.

The western kingbird is an elegant bird, with a pale gray head and breast that contrasts with a lemon-yellow belly and black, white-edged tail. Unfortunately for the novice bird-watcher, there are several other very similar species of kingbirds in the West, although only Cassin's kingbird, which lacks the white tail edges of the western, is widespread.

Living as it does in a part of the continent where trees are a scarce commodity, the western kingbird has shown a quirky ability to adapt to the circumstances during the nesting season. When trees are available it nests 20 or 30 feet up, building the nest against the trunk on a supporting branch. In the absence of trees, this species has been known to nest on windmill pumps, church steeples, telephone poles and the eaves of homes.

The charge of bee-eating that is unjustly leveled against the eastern kingbird could be correctly made against the western, for about a third of this species' diet is made up of bees, wasps and hornets.

In winter, this insect-eater must migrate to warmer lands or perish, so it heads south, to Mexico and Central America. A few can be counted on to stray off-course each autumn, ending up on the East Coast to excite bird-watchers.

DISTRIBUTION AND IDENTIFICATION

PLUMAGE Gray head, throat and chest; yellow belly. Black, white-edged tail.

HABITAT Fields, ranchlands and towns.

FOOD Insects; Bees, wasps, hornets.

NEST Cup of grasses and weeds, usually lined with soft wool, feathers or hair, in trees, shrubs or buildings.

EGGS 3–5 eggs with heavy dark blotches.

SCISSOR-TAILED FLYCATCHER
TYRANNUS FORFICATUS

With its long tail plumes streaming in the breeze, the scissor-tailed flycatcher looks like some exotic creature of the jungle, instead of a common resident of the southern Plains.

One of the most beautiful birds in North America, the scissor-tail is another member of the tyrant fly-catcher family, along with both kingbirds. In fact, appearances aside, it is so closely related to the western kingbird that it has been known to hybridize with that species.

Its range is rather restricted, from Nebraska south to Texas, and the edges of New Mexico, Missouri, Arkansas and Louisiana. There is no mistaking an adult for anything else – the tail feathers more than double the bird's body length, scissoring together in flight. The body is gray, but when the flycatcher takes off, it shows a delicate salmon wash on its sides and wing linings, and a bright patch of red in each wing pit.

As if his looks weren't enough, the male performs a spectacular sky dance during courtship, a compli-cated roller-coaster of dives, loops and rolls, ac-companied by a loud cackling. The nest tree of choice is the mesquite, in which the adults assemble a loose bowl of weeds, twigs and whatever else is handy. The young do not acquire the flowing tail in their first summer, and might be mistaken for a separate species entirely, were it not for a pinkish cast on their sides.

DISTRIBUTION AND IDENTIFICATION

PLUMAGE Gray body. Salmon wash on sides and wing linings in flight; patch of red in wing pits. Long tail plumes.

HABITAT Open prairies.

FOOD Insects.

NEST Loose bowl of weeds, twigs, etc; preferably in mesquite trees.

EGGS 3–5 eggs; white with brown splotching.

Scissor-tailed flycatchers are notoriously tame around humans, often ignoring pedestrians and cars alike when they are flitting from perch to air and back again to catch insects. When one wanders out of its usual range – as happens on a regular basis – it causes a sensation, not just among naturalists, but also among passersby who usually spare little atten-tion to birds.

EASTERN PHOEBE
SAYORNIS PHOEBE

Anondescript bird with little color and a listless song, the phoebe is nevertheless a longstanding favorite of many, who are won over by its close association with humans and its early appearance in the spring, before most migrants have even left South America.

The phoebe's best field mark is not its pattern, but its habit of ceaselessly pumping its tail up and down, emphasizing its call: *fee-BEE, FEE-bee, fee-BEE*. The phoebe is one of more than a half-dozen confusing, small flycatchers in the East, but none shares its call or its tail-wagging.

The sight of a phoebe nest on the rafters of a cabin porch, on the inside lintel of a springhouse or beneath a bridge span is a common one. This species seems perfectly content to live side-by-side with people, eventually learning to ignore even a close approach. The nest is tightly made, a heavy mass of grass stems and weed blades, carefully woven together and covered with mud and an outer coat of moss. The lining is soft plant down and, where available, often includes deer hair – an excellent insulator. The female usually lays five eggs, but brown-headed cowbirds parasitize phoebe nests heavily, tossing out the phoebe eggs and laying their own instead. If the cowbird strikes before the phoebe has laid her eggs she will abandon the nest, but if the attack comes later, the phoebe is liable to be suckered by the switch, and raise the cowbird chicks as if they were her own. Sometimes, if the ploy is discovered, the phoebe will simply build another layer onto the nest, covering the cowbird eggs; one nest was found with six such layers.

During the warmer months the phoebe is an insect-eater, as all flycatchers are, but its habit of switching to berries gives it a greater flexibility in the face of cold weather. Phoebes that arrive in the North in early spring, only to find themselves caught in an unseasonable cold snap, can simply eat the berries of greenbrier, poison ivy and other plants, until the weather warms.

DISTRIBUTION AND IDENTIFICATION

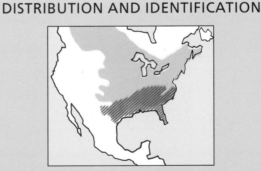

PLUMAGE Grayish-brown back with whitish underparts.

HABITAT Common in rural and residential areas.

FOOD Insects in warm weather, berries in cold.

NEST Heavy woven mass of grass stems and weed blades, covered with mud and outer coat of moss; lined with soft plant down, deer hair if available; often made in building rafters, under bridges.

EGGS 4–5 white eggs with a few scattered spots.

SAY'S PHOEBE
SAYORNIS SAYA

The western counterpart of the eastern phoebe, Say's phoebe is the only flycatcher with a cinnamon belly, making it a pleasantly easy bird to identify, compared with the rest of the flycatcher family.

Say's phoebes are found in a wide swath of open country, from central Alaska, down through the Canadian prairie and across most of the American West, where the horizon stretches unbroken by forests. An open-country bird, Say's phoebe is found in sagebrush flats, grasslands and arid hills, where it hunts insects from low perches.

Like the eastern phoebe, Say's shows a fondness for nesting around people, often constructing its nest in buildings, abandoned or otherwise. The nest is shaped like an eastern phoebe's, but – because water is often hard to find in its dry habitat – Say's phoebe uses no mud or moss to mortar it together. In the days before widespread human settlement in the West, it is likely that canyon walls and cave mouths were the nest sites of preference, and many Say's phoebes still opt for such places. Considering the long occupancy of the Southwest by adobe-building Indians, though, it's a good guess that the phoebe has been co-habitating with people for many, many centuries.

This species' call, often described as melancholy, is a soft *phee-ar*. In the spring, males sing a rapid *pit-tsee-ar* repeatedly, often following it with a trilling song given from flight.

Insects, especially grasshoppers, beetles, wasps and bees, form almost all of the Say's phoebe's food. Such a diet is high in roughage, and so this species has the odd (for a songbird) habit of ejecting a pellet comprising of the chitonous shells and body parts of the bugs it has eaten.

DISTRIBUTION AND IDENTIFICATION

PLUMAGE Grayish brown with cinnamon belly.

HABITAT Open country, especially sagebrush flats, grasslands and arid hills.

FOOD Insects, especially grasshoppers, beetles, wasps, bees.

NEST Heavy woven mass of grass stems and weed blades; often made in buildings, but found in canyon walls and cave mouths.

EGGS 4–5 white eggs, sometimes finely spotted.

TREE SWALLOW
TACHYCINETA BICOLOR

One of the first migrants to test the fickle spring weather each year is the tree swallow, returning to its haunt along waterways. Like the eastern phoebe, this is an insect-eating species that can switch its diet to berries, thus lengthening the amount of time it can spend on its breeding grounds.

About six inches long, adult tree swallows are white below and iridescent blue-green above. They are consummate acrobats, cutting snappy loops and dives as they fly. Primarily northerners, tree swallows are found from the arctic south to Maryland, the Ohio Valley, New Mexico and California, but are absent from the Plains and most of the South.

Prime tree swallow habitat usually includes wide expanses of water, like fresh- and salt-water marshes, lakes and rivers, with plenty of dead trees for nesting. Tree swallows cannot chop their own nest cavities, and so are at the mercy of woodpeckers and tree diseases to provide for them. Little wonder, then, that artificial nest boxes are readily accepted.

Only the hardest-hearted wouldn't appreciate the sight of tree swallows outfitting their nest. White feathers are the preferred lining, and a handful of chicken feathers, released into a brisk spring wind, will send the local tree swallows into a frenzy of collection. Once nesting begins, the male will drive off any other tree swallows that come too close, although such territoriality seems to break down in areas with a high concentration of nest holes, such as a stand of dead, woodpecker-riddled trees at the edge of a marsh.

In fall along the East Coast, hundreds of thousands of tree swallows descend on the close-crowded thickets of bayberry and poison ivy near the dunes, filling up on the abundant berries. Eventually, the flocks migrate south, wintering from the Gulf Coast down through Central America.

DISTRIBUTION AND IDENTIFICATION

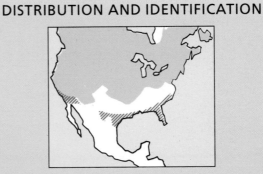

PLUMAGE White below, iridescent blue-green above.

HABITAT Open country near fresh- and salt-water marshes, lakes and rivers; areas with dead trees.

FOOD Insects and berries.

NEST In holes of dead trees, preferably lined with white feathers; accept artificial nest boxes.

EGGS 4–6 white eggs.

PURPLE MARTIN
PROGNE SUBIS

The lives of people and martins have been intertwined for a long time – exactly how long, no one knows. When Europeans first sailed to North America, however, they found that many Indian tribes took great pains to attract martin colonies to their villages, where the birds' insect-eating abilities were certainly appreciated. The Indians would choose a sapling in the village, lop off its topmost branches, and suspend hollow gourds in which the martins would nest.

Today, fancy "apartment" houses, some costing hundreds of dollars, are snapped up by people anxious to have a martin colony near their home – but simple gourds still work. Apartment or gourd, they both point up the reliance purple martins place on man-made housing: only in the rarest cases (and most remote locations) do martins revert to "primitive" nest sites, like woodpecker cavities.

The purple martin is North America's largest swallow, eight inches long and much more robust than the continent's other species. Males are a deep, glossy purple all over, while females and immature birds have a gray breast. Their talent as mosquito-catchers is widely known – and perhaps a bit exaggerated – because in fact they feed on almost any flying insect.

The spring migration usually occurs in three waves. First, a few males arrive, perhaps acting as scouts, only to leave again. Shortly thereafter, the rest of the males appear, portending the arrival of the

DISTRIBUTION AND IDENTIFICATION

PLUMAGE Male, glossy deep purple all over; female and immatures have gray breast.

HABITAT Open country, farmland, or residential areas where nest boxes provided.

FOOD Flying insects, such as mosquitoes.

NEST Reliant on manmade housing, e.g., hollow gourds, artificial houses; rarely, woodpecker cavities in trees.

EGGS 4–6 pure white eggs.

females usually a week or two later.

Sadly, martin colonies are declining in many areas of the country. Competition for nesting holes is an important reason; house sparrows and starlings start nesting weeks before the martins even return in the spring, and easily bully this less aggressive bird. Pesticide use has also been implicated, both in North America and, to a greater extent, on the martins' wintering grounds in South America.

BARN SWALLOW
HIRUNDO RUSTICA

It is hard to imagine country life without barn swallows, because they are so much a part of rural existence in almost all of the U.S. and Canada – swooping above newly mown hay fields, perched in noisy rows on telephone wires or ferrying food to their young in a nest above the barn door.

Barn swallows are undemanding in habitat and nest site. Equally at home in the arid Southwest or catching blackflies above a Quebec bog, they are most commonly associated with agricultural land. The major requirement of any locale is that it offer insects, and lots of them. Dedicated amateur biologists of the late 19th century, endeavoring to prove the economic worth of songbirds, laboriously cataloged the stomach contents of almost every species; one fellow analyzed 467 barn swallow stomachs and concluded that flies comprised 39.49% of the birds' diet, with beetles (15.6%), wasps (12.8%) and ants (9.8%) among the runners-up. With a grand flourish of ethnocentrism, he pronounced the swallow "beneficial".

Anyone who has spent a lazy summer afternoon watching them knows that the value of swallows transcends economics. They are beautiful birds; the adults have a shiny blue back and head, a deep chestnut throat and a buff belly, as well as the deeply forked tail that is this species' trademark. They call constantly, in flight and while perched, a lively chatter of "chips" and twittering that never stops. While not quite as social as most swallows, they do feed in large, shifting flocks, perhaps drawn to the same area by an abundance of food, and occasionally nest in colonies.

Soon after they return in the spring, pairs of barn swallows scout out nest locations. Almost any flat, sheltered spot will be considered – barn rafters, sheds or the lip under a farmyard electrical light, for instance. Swallows are quick to investigate any dark opening, and the person who accidentally leaves the garage open for the day may return in the evening to find a half-built nest on the raised door. The nest itself is a messy semicircle of straw and grass, cemented with mud that the swallows laboriously collect in tiny balls.

DISTRIBUTION AND IDENTIFICATION

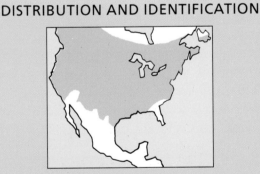

PLUMAGE Shiny blue back and head, chestnut throat and buff belly. Deeply forked tail.

HABITAT Rural areas, mostly on agricultural land.

FOOD Insects.

NEST Messy semicircle of straw and grass, cemented with mud; found in any flat, sheltered spot (e.g. barn rafters, sheds).

EGGS 4–5 eggs; white with fine spotting at large end.

SCRUB JAY
APHELOCOMA COERULESCENS

Most birds have contiguous ranges – that is, they occur in areas that form connected masses. Not so the scrub jay. This animated species has two distinct populations: one across much of the West, and an isolated subspecies in Florida.

The separation has had an effect on the Florida birds, which have developed a white forehead that their western cousins lack. Even more interesting, the young of the Florida race help their parents care for subsequent broods of babies, an all-for-one, one-for-all behavior that doesn't occur in the West, and which may last for two or more years.

East or West, a scrub jay is an attractive bird, with a blue head, back and tail, gray breast and a white throat set off by a necklace of dark feathers – a throat that may be dull gray in birds from the interior mountains. They measure about 11 inches – pretty much standard for jays of any species.

The scrub jay likes brushy habitat – scrub oak and pinyons in the West, and thickets of oak and palmetto in Florida. They are common in residential areas, foraging for insects, seeds, nuts, berries, small frogs and lizards, and can be enticed to come to feeders for sunflower seeds, suet and cracked corn.

The scrub jay's neatly constructed nest is built in low trees and shrubs, and among Florida birds may involve a loose colony of up to a half-dozen pairs. Scrub jays are notably fearless when incubating – one wildlife photographer I know finally asked a friend to hold a female that simply would not stay off her nest long enough for him to photograph her eggs.

DISTRIBUTION AND IDENTIFICATION

PLUMAGE Blue upperparts, gray below , with white wing and tail markings.

HABITAT Forests and woodlots.

FOOD Wide variety of seeds, nuts, berries, insects and other animal food; whole corn, peanut kernels, suet at feeder.

NEST Sticks laid together as foundation, softer materials for inner cup, finished with lining of root-lets; in tree branches high above ground.

EGGS 4–5 eggs; buffy with dark brown spots.

BLUE JAY
CYANOCITTA CRISTATA

Smart and sassy, the blue jay takes no guff from anyone. A cat that tries to sneak through its domain is greeted with a piercing *jaaay, jaaay, jaaay*, and if it should approach the bird's nest too closely, it will be driven away with lightning-fast attacks and hammering blows from the jay's powerful beak.

In the forests and woodlots from the western Plains on east, there can be no mistaking the blue jay for another species, for it is the only blue bird in its range with a crest. In the eastern Rockies, where it is found with the similar Stellar's jay, look for the blue jay's white wing and tail markings, and the Stellar's black crest and head.

The blue jay is one of the most common winter visitors to bird feeders, and while its color and vivacious personality make it a lively addition to a winter's day, it can be a bully, keeping smaller song-birds away from the food. Many bird-watchers solve this problem by setting up a special blue jay feeding area, away from their regular feeders, and stocking it with whole corn, peanut kernels and suet.

In spring, the blue jay pair will select a tree branch high above the ground. Starting with a base of twigs, both male and female (indistinguishable as such except to each other) work on the nest, lacing the sticks to form a solid foundation, then progressing to finer and softer materials for the inner cup, finishing with a lining of rootlets. In years past the blue jay was viewed as something of a terror during the breeding season, accused of habitually stealing the eggs and chicks of other birds. While such depredations certainly do happen (the blue jay is, after all, an opportunistic feeder), the magnitude hardly justifies the wrath with which this beautiful bird was condemned.

DISTRIBUTION AND IDENTIFICATION

PLUMAGE Blue head, back and tail; gray breast. White throat set off by dark "necklace" (dull gray in some). Florida subspecies, white forehead.
HABITAT Brushy areas; scrub oak and pinyons in western subspecies, thickets of oak and palmetto in Florida subspecies.
FOOD Insects, seeds, nuts, berries, small frogs and lizards; sunflower seeds, suet and cracked corn at feeder.
NEST Neatly built in low trees and shrubs.
EGGS 3–4 eggs; either pale green with dark green spotting, or grayish-white with red-brown freckling.

AMERICAN CROW
CORVUS BRACHYRHYNCHOS

Arguably the most intelligent bird in North America, the common crow has thrived in the face of civilization because of its brains, its adaptability and its willingness to survive on whatever fate throws its way. Along the coast, it may feast on dead fish and fresh crabs. In suburbia, crows raid garbage cans and scavenge for French fries on the parking lots of fast-food restaurants. In farm country, they eat grain, insects, carrion, reptiles and amphibians, small mammals, bird eggs – in short, just about anything.

Shining purple where the sun glints off its smooth, black feathers, a crow is a handsome bird. More so than small songbirds, it seems to be able to convey expression in the cock of its head, or the posture of its body. A flock, playfully diving at each other in aerial roughhousing, is the epitome of enjoyment, but let them spot a great horned owl, and they become the very picture of murderous rage as they mercilessly harass the larger predator.

Eighteen inches from the tip of its powerful beak to the end of its tail, the crow is the biggest all-black bird in most of its range, exceeded in size only by the wilderness-dwelling raven. American crows are found from the northern treeline south and from coast to coast, and are absent only from the extreme Southwest. Two very similar species have much smaller ranges – the fish crow of the eastern coast, and the northwestern crow of the British Columbian and Alaskan coastline.

Through much of the year, crows are flock birds, sometimes roosting together by the tens of thousands. During the breeding season, however, the pairs live solitary lives. Nest building begins early in spring, with both adults working to finish the rather bulky assemblage of sticks, vines and twigs. Ironically, old crow nests are often used in subsequent years by great horned owls, which crows hate with a passion justified by the regular attacks the owls make on crow roosts.

DISTRIBUTION AND IDENTIFICATION

PLUMAGE Black; shows purple cast in sunlight.

HABITAT Widespread; open woodland, farm country, coastal areas and suburbia.

FOOD Just about anything, from dead fish to grain, insects, reptiles, small mammals, bird eggs.

NEST Bulky assemblage of sticks, vines, twigs and bark, built high in trees.

EGGS 4–5 eggs; bluish-green, heavily spotted with brown.

TUFTED TITMOUSE
PARUS BICOLOR

Titmice are among the first birds to breed in the spring. In the north, males can be heard singing their warbling *peter peter peter* song on mornings when the temperature is well below freezing, and the pair has usually at least started with nesting by the end of March. The holes of downy and hairy woodpeckers are most often used, lined with hair and fur to cushion the eggs. In collecting that fur, titmice have a reputation for doggedness; they have been known to pluck it from live animals, and in at least one celebrated case, from the face of a bearded man.

Like their close relations, the chickadees, the sexes among titmice are identical – sparrow-sized, gray birds with white underparts and pert crests. The only color on them is just a touch of peach on the sides and flanks.

Tufted titmice are nonmigratory, living in deciduous forests and groves from the Gulf Coast and southern Plains up through the Great Lakes states and into southern New England.

During the winter, many titmice move out of the deep woods and into residential areas, where they are among the easiest birds to attract to feeders. Suet, cracked corn and peanut butter are eaten, but by far the best food is sunflower seed – especially black, or oil, sunflower, a smaller, more nutritious variety than the standard striped seed.

Even while feeding, they keep a wary eye out for danger, and should a sharp-shinned hawk suddenly appear, it is usually a titmouse that sounds the first (and loudest) alarm – a piercing, almost screaming note repeated every second or two until the threat has passed.

DISTRIBUTION AND IDENTIFICATION

PLUMAGE Gray, with white underparts and pert crests. Touch of peach on sides and flanks.

HABITAT Deciduous forests and groves; residential areas in winter.

FOOD Insects and seeds; sunflower seeds, suet, cracked corn and peanut butter at feeder.

NEST Holes of woodpeckers, lined with hair and fur.

EGGS 4–6 eggs; white with fine brown spots.

BLACK-CAPPED CHICKADEE
PARUS ATRICAPILLUS

As the robin is the bird of spring, so then is the black-capped chickadee usually first thought of when winter birds come to mind.

A flock of chickadees enlivens any day, but especially when the cold winds are howling and life seems to have deserted the woods. Weighing only a few ounces, a chickadee is an irrepressible bundle of energy as it darts from branch to branch, giving its trademark *chick-a-dee-dee-dee* call as it goes.

Chickadees are enjoyed also for their trusting nature. Anyone with a little patience can train these sprites to come to the hand for food. Simply stand near the feeder for a time each day, hand outstretched, with sunflower seeds in one's hand. At first the chickadees will hang back, scolding, but before too many sessions have passed, the boldest of the flock will flash in, grab a seed and zip away again.

When warm weather returns, the chickadee flocks break up, deserting the feeders for the breeding season. Among small songbirds, chickadees are unusual in that they often excavate their own nest cavities, instead of using abandoned woodpecker holes (although they are not above using such a hole if the opportunity presents itself). The mated pair chooses an old, rotting stump, often held together by nothing more than the bark casing. Both adults work on the hole, tearing away chunks of soft wood fibers in their beaks; when one pops out of the hole with a mouthful, it appears to be wearing a pale mustache.

When finished, the nest cavity is lined with moss, feathers, deer hair, plant down – almost any warm, soft material the chickadees can find. While the female incubates, her mate will bring insects to her to eat. Later, when there are a half-dozen or more hungry mouths in the nest, both parents will hunt.

DISTRIBUTION AND IDENTIFICATION

PLUMAGE Gray back with black cap and bib; white cheeks and underparts.

HABITAT Wooded areas, swamplands and parks.

FOOD Insects, berries, seeds; sunflower seeds at feeder.

NEST Self-excavated cavity, often in rotting stump, lined with moss, feathers, deer hair, plant down.

EGGS 6–8 eggs; white with rufous spotting.

MOUNTAIN CHICKADEE
PARUS GAMBELI

In the high forests of subalpine fir and spruce that cloak the sides of the western peaks, the mountain chickadee is one of the birds most quickly noticed. With its constant *tsick-adee-adee-adee* call and frenetic habits, it is a favorite of high-country hikers, who will find this bird breeding at elevations of up to 10,000 feet.

In size and shape, the mountain chickadee is identical to the black-capped, which sticks to lower elevations. A white eye-stripe and pale gray flanks distinguish it easily, however, and its song, while obviously a chickadee's, is lower and hoarser.

In winter, the mountain chickadee forsakes the harsh hills for lower, somewhat milder climates, and in some areas is a common feeder bird.

Perhaps because of its high-altitude habitat, the mountain chickadee hasn't been studied as much as most songbirds, and information on its habits is scarce. It is a cavity nester, and apparently does not excavate its own hole, using woodpecker choppings

DISTRIBUTION AND IDENTIFICATION

PLUMAGE Identical to black-capped chickadee, but with pale gray flanks and white eye-stripe.

HABITAT High forests of subalpine fir and spruce; lower regions in winter.

FOOD Insects, berries, seeds; feeder bird in some areas.

NEST In tree cavity, usually in rotting stump; sometimes woodpecker holes, knotholes.

EGGS 7 or 8 white eggs with scattered brown spotting.

or knotholes instead. Like other chickadee species, the nest is most often in a rotting stump.

For such a tiny bird, mountain chickadees lay exceptionally large clutches of eggs; the average is nine, and nests with 12 or more have been recorded. So high a reproductive rate speaks volumes for the dangers a chickadee faces, because only by raising so many young can the species keep abreast with the losses from weather, predators and other natural hazards.

WHITE-BREASTED NUTHATCH
SITTA CAROLINENSIS

The nuthatch certainly earns the rural nickname "upside-down bird." Although perfectly capable of perching upright, its typical pose is clinging to the trunk of a tree head down, descending in herky-jerky movements.

Why upside-down? Food is the answer. Downy woodpeckers, which inhabit the same forests as nuthatches, climb trees rightside-up, probing for bugs under the bark. Biologists guess that by descending the tree head-first, nuthatches are able to spot insects that have been missed by woodpeckers, thus opening up an untapped food supply.

White-breasted nuthatches have a creamy face and breast, blue-gray back and a black cap (gray in females). Both sexes have at least some rusty coloration between the legs and under the tail. Its call is a distinctive, nasal *yank, yank, yank,* but it is so soft that it can usually be heard only at fairly short ranges.

Surprisingly for a bird with such a strong bill, nuthatches do not excavate their own nest holes, nor do they use those of woodpeckers. Instead, they seek out knotholes and other natural cavities, which they line with shredded bark, grass, leaves and fur.

The odd name "nuthatch" is apparently a corruption of an older, European name, "nut-hack." Its appropriateness is evident when one watches a white-breasted nuthatch wedge an acorn in a handy crack, then patiently chop away at it.

Altogether, there are four species of nuthatches in North America, including the red-breasted nuthatch, widespread in northern and mountainous areas in summer, and in conifer forests continent-wide in winter. It is smaller than the white-breasted, with a russet belly and a white eye-stripe. The pygmy nuthatch of the West is about the same size, as is the brown-headed nuthatch, common in pine forests in the Southeast.

DISTRIBUTION AND IDENTIFICATION

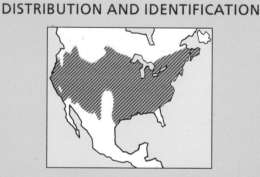

PLUMAGE Creamy face and breast; blue-gray back and black cap (female, gray cap). Rusty color between legs and under tail.

HABITAT Forests.

FOOD Insects, nuts and seeds.

NEST In knotholes and other cavities; lined with shredded bark, grass, leaves and fur.

EGGS 7–8 eggs; white with fine brown spotting.

HOUSE WREN
TROGLODYTES AEDON

John James Audubon, the great 19th-century bird artist, painted a pair of house wrens nesting in an old felt hat, hung from a branch. Such odd places are the norm for wrens, which have been recorded nesting in stranger spots than perhaps any other bird – mailboxes, drainpipes, tin cans, cow skulls, even the pockets of shirts hung out on the clothesline to dry.

Because they are so open-minded when it comes to picking a home, it is obvious why house wrens are the easiest birds to lure into an artificial nest box. Almost any sort will do, but boxes made specifically for wrens are rather small, with a one-inch-wide entrance hole.

House wrens are small brown birds, less than five inches long, with short tails that they frequently cock skyward when they perch. They are, quite literally, a "garden bird," most at home around the flowerbeds, shade trees and shrubs of backyards. Highly migratory, wrens feed almost exclusively on insects.

As with many songbirds, the male wrens arrive a few weeks before the females. They waste little time, and immediately start to build so-called "cock nests,"

masses of twigs stuffed in any likely cavity. When his mate returns, he will show each nest to her – but it is rare for her to accept his work, usually preferring to build her own. Most likely, the cock nests serve a courtship function, and are not really meant to be used.

A male house wren's bubbling song is at once advertisement and warning, reaffirming the bond with his mate while warning neighboring males to stay clear of his territory. Should the local wren population have more females than males, he may take a second or even third mate, with each female responsible for most of the chick-rearing.

Chances are, the wren that returns to your backyard is the one that nested there the year before. Studies have shown that wrens are very faithful to their breeding territories, and return as often as their short lifespans allow. The young, on the other hand, scatter widely, searching for vacant areas where they can claim a parcel for themselves.

DISTRIBUTION AND IDENTIFICATION

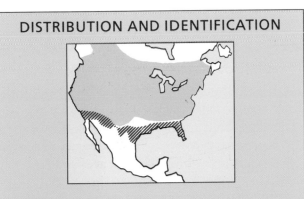

PLUMAGE Brown with short tail.

HABITAT Backyard gardens.

FOOD Insects.

NEST Masses of twigs stuffed anywhere, from tin cans and old hats to drainpipes and mailboxes; take to nest boxes.

EGGS 6 or 7 eggs; buffy with heavy russet speckling.

BEWICK'S WREN
THRYOMANES BEWICKII

Despite more than a century of intensive study, there is much to learn about North America's birds, particularly the dynamics of changing populations.

The Bewick's wren is a good example. It is, for the most part, a southern species, found in greatest abundance from the upper Midwest, down through the American heartland and west to the Pacific coast, nudging up into British Columbia. Arthur Cleveland Bent, whose monumental, 26-volume "Life History" series remains the best compendium of information on the continent's birds, noted 40 years ago that it had greatly expanded its range northward around the turn of the century.

DISTRIBUTION AND IDENTIFICATION

PLUMAGE Rufous back, gray belly, and white eye-stripe.

HABITAT Backyard gardens.

FOOD Primarily insects.

NEST Occasionally in natural cavities in trees, but usually in bird houses or other man-made sites.

EGGS 5–10 eggs, wreathed at large end with brownish spotting.

But like a tide that rises and ebbs, Bewick's wren has disappeared from many of the areas it had expanded into. Once found in scattered locations as far north as central Pennsylvania, the species now seems to be retreating to its original range.

Something changed, certainly, to cause both the expansion and the more recent contraction. It may have been habitat, it may have been a changing relationship with the more common house wren and Carolina wren. There are guesses, but no firm answers.

Fortunately, Bewick's wren (named for John James Audubon's English engraver), is still common across much of the country. It is very much a "house" wren, taking well to backyard gardens and to manmade birdboxes. Slightly larger than a house wren, it has a much longer tail, which it fans and flicks constantly. Because of the Bewick's white eye-stripe, many people confuse it with the Carolina wren of the East, which has an overall rufous color, compared with the gray belly of the Bewick's.

GOLDEN-CROWNED KINGLET
REGULUS SATRAPA

Among North American birds, only the humming-birds are smaller than golden-crowned kinglets, tiny sprites barely four inches long. Trusting and engaging, they look like nothing quite so much as a fluffy ball with a beak and tail.

Both sexes are greenish-gray above, with gray underparts and white wingbars. A black cap is split by a yellow crown that, in the male, has a bright orange center. Unfortunately, this drop of brilliant color is usually hidden by surrounding yellow feathers, so determining sex can be tricky.

The species is found continent-wide, except for the arctic. It lives year-round in coniferous forests in the Northeast, Appalachians and West, and in winter spreads out into the Plains and South, sticking to forested areas.

A branch high in a spruce tree is usually picked for the nest site. Moss and lichen are woven among the small twigs that protrude down from the branch, to form a globular nest with an entrance hole at the top. The female does all the nest building herself, but the male assists her when the chicks have hatched.

Sometimes, human actions have an unintended positive effect on birds, and such has been the case in some areas with the golden-crowned kinglet. In New York, for instance, kinglets were originally confined to the higher elevations of the Adirondack and Catskill mountains, where dense spruce forests grew.

But with the advent of conservation plantings in the 1930s, dense stands of spruce and pine were planted widely for erosion control and reforestation. Its habitat greatly expanded, golden-crowned kinglets can now be found breeding in many areas of the state, even at fairly low elevations. The same story has been repeated in many other regions as well.

DISTRIBUTION AND IDENTIFICATION

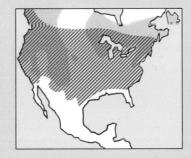

PLUMAGE Greenish-gray above, gray underparts; white wingbars. Black cap split by yellow crown (orange center in males).

HABITAT Coniferous forests.

FOOD Insects.

NEST Globular, with top entrance hole, of moss and lichen woven among small twigs that protrude from branch; usually high in spruce trees.

EGGS 6–8 eggs, white splotched with brown.

EASTERN BLUEBIRD
SIALIA SIALIS

In the horse-and-buggy days of the 1800s, the eastern bluebird was the most beloved country bird in the U.S. – the common harbinger of spring, the sweet-voiced singer that serenaded farmers from every fence wire or treetop.

But in later years, the bluebird population suffered greatly. The wooden fenceposts in which they nested were rapidly replaced by metal stakes. Pesticides reduced the insects on which they fed (and in many cases killed the bluebirds directly). Starlings and house sparrows which were introduced to North America bullied the surviving bluebirds from their few remaining nest holes.

DISTRIBUTION AND IDENTIFICATION

PLUMAGE Male: deep blue on back, head, wings and tail, with rufous throat and breast, white belly. Female duller, wings tinged with brown, head gray. Immatures have spotted breasts.

HABITAT Open areas with scattered trees.

FOOD Insects.

NEST Primarily take to artificial nest boxes, also natural cavities and old woodpecker holes.

EGGS 4–5 pale blue eggs.

Thankfully, the bluebird's prospects have brightened considerably, thanks to the general public. Millions of bluebird houses, built by Scout groups, bird watchers and environmentally minded homeowners, have created a wealth of breeding locations, and the birds have responded in fine fashion. Today, the welcome sight of a bluebird is again commonplace in many areas.

A member of the thrush family, the eastern bluebird is, in fact, found as far west as eastern Montana, Wyoming and Arizona. Males are deep blue on the back, head, wings and tail, with a rufous throat and breast, and a white belly. A female bluebird is duller; her blue wings are tinged with brown, and her head is gray. Immatures, like all young thrushes, have spotted breasts.

Repeated experimentation has shown that bluebird boxes should have entrance holes no larger than one-and-a-half inches (to exclude starlings), and should be about 18 inches deep to thwart cats. Place the box on a post between four and six feet high, facing south or east to avoid wind-blown rain. Bluebirds like to nest in open areas with scattered trees, so fencerows, parks and rural backyards are all prime locations.

MOUNTAIN BLUEBIRD
SIALIA CURRUCOIDES

In the foothills and ranges of the West, where lodge-pole pines, aspens and cottonwoods mingle with sagebrush and meadows, the mountain bluebird is a common summer resident.

The male looks like a piece of the sky given wings – a beautiful shade of cerulean blue, with pale blue underparts. The female is much drabber, but her wings and tail are edged with blue.

Mountain bluebirds are common roadside birds in many areas, especially the males, which often claim fenceposts as territory markers, darting out from their base to snatch insects or chase interlopers.

Wooden fenceposts also serve as handy nest locations, if they have decayed to form a hole, or if woodpeckers have been chopping at them; the same goes for trees and dead snags. Both sexes help to finish the nest with a fairly simple lining of grasses and weed leaves. The five or six eggs are usually pale blue, but are sometimes plain white.

Except in the highest locations, mountain bluebirds raise two broods of young each summer. The babies have a terrifically high metabolism, and must

DISTRIBUTION AND IDENTIFICATION

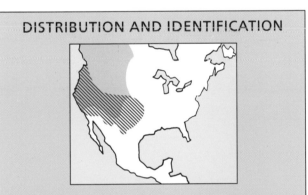

PLUMAGE Male, cerulean blue with pale blue underparts. Female drabber, with wings and tail edged with blue.

HABITAT Foothills and ranges of West.

FOOD Insects.

NEST Often wooden fenceposts with holes; also in trees and dead snags; simply lined with grasses and weed leaves.

EGGS 4–5 eggs; pale blue or white.

be fed endlessly. One naturalist, observing a mountain bluebird nest on the slopes of Mt. Rainier, noted that the adults brought food on average every 2.4 minutes, for a total of nearly 375 trips each day. With such a constant feast, the young are able to double their weight each day during their first week of life, and by 14 days of age are fully feathered – marked, as with other young bluebirds, by numerous spots.

North America has yet a third species of this colorful group, the western bluebird – similar in pattern to the eastern, but with a blue, rather than chestnut, throat. Much of its range overlaps that of the mountain bluebird, but it is generally found at lower elevations.

WOOD THRUSH
HYLOCICHLA MUSTELINA

In the soft half-light of dawn, when the forest is still largely quiet, the wood thrush tilts back its head to sing. The result, many believe, is one of the most beautiful of all bird songs, a liquid cascade of notes that ring through the still air in flute-like couplets: *Ee-o-lee . . . Ee-o-lay.*

The songster itself blends easily with the surrounding forest. The sexes are identical, both bearing a reddish-brown head, brown back and white breast with black spots. In the mature forests of the East, wood thrushes are common, hunting through fallen leaves and among low branches for the insects and berries on which they feed.

The nest is usually built in the forest (although shady gardens are occasionally chosen), about 10 feet off the ground in the branches of a tree. The thrush always starts with a layer of leaves, then uses mud, grass, bark and more leaves to form the cup, ending up with a nest that looks very much like a robin's – with one important exception. If a wood thrush can find white paper, pieces of cloth or cellophane, this trash will be added to the nest, sometimes creating a bizarre streamered effect. Where manmade materials aren't present, the thrush may use light-colored weed stalks or leaves. The eggs are similar in shape and color to a robin's – the norm for most North American thrushes.

For centuries, the greatest hazards facing any migratory bird came during the twice-annual migration itself. But for the wood thrush, as for many of our common forest birds, the rampant destruction of Central American forests threatens their continued survival. Increasingly, songbirds returning to their traditional wintering grounds have found fields and logging operations, rather than rain forests. It is unlikely that they can adapt to such drastic changes in their environment, and only time will tell if the thrush's daybreak song will eventually fall silent.

DISTRIBUTION AND IDENTIFICATION

PLUMAGE Reddish-brown head, brown back and white breast with black spots. Tail olive-brown.

HABITAT Mature forested land.

FOOD Insects and berries.

NEST Layers of, first, leaves, then mud, grass, bark and more leaves to form cup; white paper or cloth often used as "streamers"; built in tree branches some 10 ft above ground.

EGGS 3–4 blue-green eggs.

HERMIT THRUSH
CATHARUS GUTTATUS

Deep, moist forests of conifers – the kind of woods where wild orchids grow in damp soil, and even the sunlight is soft and green – are home to the hermit thrush, a species that lives up to its name.

At first glance, the hermit thrush and wood thrush look very much alike, with the same plump, robinish shape and ground-hugging habits. But whereas the wood thrush's head is rusty and its tail olive-brown, the hermit thrush reverses the pattern. The breast is also buffier on the hermit thrush, and the spots more diffuse. The songs of the two species are also different: the hermit thrush sings a long series of rising and falling notes that justifies its genus name, *Catharus*, or pure.

On a map, the hermit thrush's range has three prongs – across the boreal forests of Canada and into New England and the Appalachians; down the Rockies and through the West to the Pacific coast; and north through British Columbia and into Alaska. During the breeding season this species is retiring and must be sought out in order to be seen; indeed, its lovely song of clear notes is usually the only hint of its presence. The nest is built on the ground, frequently in boggy locations, and is hidden from above by tree roots or low-hanging branches.

Unlike most other thrushes, which clear out of North America for the winter, the hermit thrush spends the cold winter fairly far north, often retreat-

DISTRIBUTION AND IDENTIFICATION

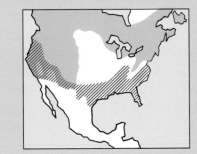

PLUMAGE Head olive-brown, tail russet; breast buffier than wood thrush's and spots more diffuse.

HABITAT Deep, moist forests of conifers; swamps and wet thickets in winter.

FOOD Berries in winter; primarily insects in summer.

NEST Cup of twigs, moss and grass, usually built on the ground, frequently in boggy locales; hidden from above by tree roots or low-hanging branches.

EGGS 3–4 pale blue eggs.

ing no further than Pennsylvania and the Ohio Valley. Swamps and wet thickets are the preferred winter habitat, in part because such areas are rich in berries – greenbriers, Virginia creeper, poison ivy and dogwood, among others. In some parts of the South, where hermit thrushes are only seen during the winter, this species was known as the "swamp robin."

AMERICAN ROBIN
TURDUS MIGRATORIUS

No other bird is known by as many people in North America as this familiar thrush, whose orange breast can be seen on lawns from Alaska to Florida, and almost everywhere in between.

So firmly is the robin associated with farmlands and residential areas, in fact, that it comes as something of a shock to see one in a truly wild setting – above timberline in the Rockies, for example.

Its wide range is ample testimony to this species' adaptability, as is its diet. Although their taste for earthworms is legendary, robins will eat a wide variety of invertebrate and plant foods, including slugs, grasshoppers, caterpillars, beetles and lots of berries and fruit.

Robins have two main calls, a lilting song described as *cheerily, cheerup, cheerio,* voiced most often at daybreak and evening, and a "laughing call" that serves as both a warning and a call note.

A robin's nest is a well-crafted bowl of grass and mud, solidly constructed in the crotch of a tree branch, beneath an awning or in a porch trellis. The eggs – four is the usual number – are pale blue, with just a hint of green; the fact that "robin's-egg blue" is a common color description is only further proof of how well-known the species is.

The chicks hatch after a two-week incubation period, and almost constant feedings give the babies the energy they need for rapid growth. Within 14 days they will have sprouted feathers and will be out of the nest, wearing spotted breasts that will fade to solid orange by late autumn.

DISTRIBUTION AND IDENTIFICATION

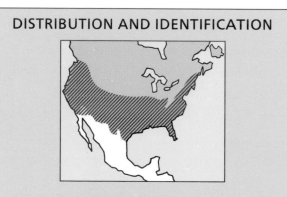

PLUMAGE Blackish head and dark back; orange breast and yellow bill.

HABITAT Farmlands and residential areas.

FOOD Earthworms, as well as a variety of invertebrate and plant foods, e.g., slugs, beetles, berries, fruit.

NEST Well-crafted bowl of grass and mud, built in crotches of tree branches, trellises, beneath awnings.

EGGS 4–5 blue-green eggs.

Because most songbirds leave the nest before they can fly well (if at all), many people mistakenly believe the chicks have been abandoned by their parents. Wild orphans are really very rare, and when confronted with such an erstwhile waif, the best course is to simply leave it alone. The chances are very good that the parents are nearby, waiting to return.

GRAY CATBIRD
DUMETELLA CAROLINENSIS

To be "sitting in the catbird seat," according to the old country saying, is to be in a very good position, to have life going well for you.

Exactly what connection catbirds have to the good life is unclear, for this common bird of thickets and hedges faces the same hazards that threaten any creature – predators, food shortages, disease and loss of habitat. Perhaps it has to do with the catbird's brash personality, since this is a bird that speaks its mind at every opportunity.

Smaller and slimmer than a robin, a catbird is sooty gray, with a black cap and a patch of chestnut under its long tail. The sexes are identical.

Along with the mockingbird and thrashers, it is a member of the mimic family, although the talent is poorly developed in most catbirds. The song is a grab-bag of original notes and imitated bird songs, some musical, some not, all interspersed with liberal doses of a strikingly cat like mew that gives the species its name.

Catbirds are first-class scolds, cussing out intruders from a safe hiding place deep in a multiflora rose hedge or chokecherry stand. Birders have found that a soft "pishing" sound, made with the lips, drives catbirds to paroxysms of anger, sometimes bringing them to within a few feet of one's face, bobbing up and down and lashing their tails in outrage.

The nest is built in the same dense thickets where the birds spend most of their time. Although there are some exceptions, including pairs that nest on the ground, almost all catbird nests are found in low shrubs and briar tangles.

Once out of the nest, the young graduate from an all-insect diet to one that includes plenty of berries and fruit. In season, they will eat wild grapes, the fruit of mountain ash, greenbrier, mulberries, elderberries and strawberries. In late summer, ripe pokeberries are greedily eaten – a fruit so intensely purple it stains even the birds' droppings.

DISTRIBUTION AND IDENTIFICATION

PLUMAGE Sooty gray, with black cap and patch of chestnut under long tail.

HABITAT Thickets and hedges

FOOD Insects, berries and fruit, including wild grapes, mulberries, strawberries, pokeberries.

NEST Shaggy mass of twigs, bark, grass and leaves, built in dense thickets, in low shrubs and briar tangles.

EGGS 3–4 blue-green eggs.

NORTHERN MOCKINGBIRD
MIMUS POLYGLOTTOS

To call this bird the "northern" mockingbird is correct in a strict, ornithological sense, because there are related species farther south (in the Bahamas, for instance). But in the United States, the mockingbird is primarily a Southerner, as much a part of that landscape as magnolia blossoms.

Interestingly, the mockingbird has made a significant, northward expansion in the 20th century. Once found no farther north than the Mason-Dixon line, they have pushed into Maine and the upper Midwest, and show no signs of stopping; their range in the West, on the other hand, has remained within historical boundaries. The usual reason given for the species' march north is the clearing of what, in pre-colonial days, had been solid forest. However, that vast forest had been largely fragmented by the late 1700s, so why the mocker is only now pushing into new territory remains an open question.

With its long tail and sleek shape, the mockingbird cuts an unmistakable figure. Both male and female are pale gray, darker on the wings and tail. In flight, white wing patches and outer tail feathers flash – an important field mark.

The mockingbird is best known for its song – or, rather, for its ability to borrow the songs of other birds and blend them into an endlessly changing concert. In spring, the concert can also be just plain endless; when the moon is bright, mockingbirds will sing all night long. In such circumstances, a person's enjoyment has been known to fade around, say, 3 a.m., especially if the bird is singing from a television antenna just above the bedroom window.

Like catbirds, mockingbirds eat a wide variety of fruit, berries and insects. In regions where winters are cold, mockingbirds will come to feeders, where their pugnacious character can cause problems for smaller birds. A separate feeding station, stocked with cracked corn, suet, raisins, sliced grapes, apples or oranges, may divert the mocker and restore peace.

DISTRIBUTION AND IDENTIFICATION

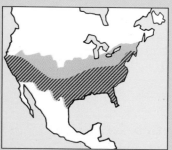

PLUMAGE Pale gray, darker on wings. White wing patches in flight. Long tail.

HABITAT Open land; farmland, parks and gardens.

FOOD Fruit, berries and insects.

NEST Large cup of twigs, lined with finer material, built in bushes or trees near ground.

EGGS 3–4 eggs; bluish with rusty-brown splotches.

BROWN THRASHER
TOXOSTOMA RUFUM

From a thicket, a bird is imitating the songs of other species – but the singer itself is invisible. How to identify it?

Simply count the number of times each phrase is repeated. A catbird usually sings each phrase only once, and rarely goes for long without *mewing*. A mockingbird generally repeats each phrase up to a half-dozen times. But if the notes are sung just twice, the hidden singer is a brown thrasher, the third of North America's common mimics.

Actually, brown thrashers are more original than their two cousins, and only rarely imitate other birds, relying instead on improvised couplets of notes, strung together in a most pleasant way.

A brown thrasher looks a little like a wood thrush that has been stretched. It has the same rusty-brown color above, a white breast and heavy streaking below, but with the mockingbird's long, lean profile. The species ranges from the East and South as far west as the foothills of the Rockies and central Texas, and up into southern Canada.

Like all of the mimics, thrashers are highly territorial during the breeding season, when males forsake the dense undergrowth to sing from high, exposed perches. The singing posts are strategically located to delineate the thrasher's territory, and where boundaries abut or overlap, constant squabbling erupts. At the core of each territory will be the nest, which may be on the ground or as high as 10 or 15 feet above it. (Early naturalists noticed that New England thrashers were much more likely to nest on the ground than those farther south or west.)

Thrashers feed extensively on insects, as well as fruits and berries; some odds and ends, including small frogs and lizards, are also occasionally taken.

DISTRIBUTION AND IDENTIFICATION

PLUMAGE Rusty-brown above, white breast and heavy streaking below.

HABITAT Areas of dense undergrowth, such as thickets and hedgerows.

FOOD Insects, fruits and berries.

NEST Large twig base with cup of grass, bark and leaves, built in thick vegetation near ground.

EGGS 3–5 eggs; pale blue with fine brown spotting.

SAGE THRASHER
OREOSCOPTES MONTANUS

Much smaller than the brown thrasher of the East, the sage thrasher is common both on sagebrush plains and around the backyards of western homes, where it sings from fenceposts or clotheslines. It is an active bird, and, after a nest full of young have fledged, it can seem that there are thrashers everywhere one looks – diving, chasing and tussling with each other.

This is the only thrasher normally found north of the Southwestern deserts. Its range extends from northern New Mexico and Arizona, west through California, Oregon and Washington, and to the eastern edges of Montana and Wyoming. It avoids mountains, sticking to the semi-arid lowlands where sage, greasewood and rabbitbush are the dominant plants.

Sage thrashers are a little more than eight inches long, and do not have either the long tail or curved beak that other western thrashers possess. The overall color is dirty brown, with a streaked, white breast; in flight, the thrasher's tail shows white corners that are helpful field marks.

Although a member of the family *Mimidae,* sage thrashers do not imitate other birds. The male's song is a long warble, usually sung from the top of a bush or during a zig-zag flight. On the rolling plains, bushes are often the highest vegetation around, and the thrasher's rough, twig nest is usually built in their low branches.

The sage thrasher spends much of the day on the ground, running with its tail cocked high as it chases insects. A grasshopper that tries to fly to safety may be nabbed on the wing. Beetles, crickets and grasshoppers make up the bulk of the thrasher's summer diet, but when the serviceberries and other wild fruits ripen, it may shift over to a vegetable menu.

Winter finds the thrasher retreating from its more northerly range, dropping south to the deserts of California, Arizona, New Mexico, Texas and Mexico.

DISTRIBUTION AND IDENTIFICATION

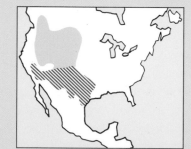

PLUMAGE Dirty brown overall, with streaked white breast. In flight tail shows white corners.

HABITAT Semi-arid lowlands, sagebrush plains and backyards.

FOOD Insects, fruits and berries.

NEST Rough twig nest in low branches of bushes.

EGGS 4–5 eggs; blue-green with heavy brown splotching.

CEDAR WAXWING
BOMBYCILLA CEDRORUM

Most songbirds spend the warm months eating little except high-protein insects, but not so the cedar waxwing. Fruit and berries comprise the major part of its diet, with insects taken almost as an after-thought. A flock of waxwings, settling into a cherry tree or mountain ash bush, will efficiently strip entire branches of fruit.

DISTRIBUTION AND IDENTIFICATION

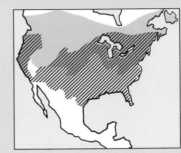

PLUMAGE Brown chest and head, lemon-yellow belly; black eye-stripe and tapered crest. Yellow band on tail tip.
HABITAT Open country with an abundance of large trees.
FOOD Fruits and berries, with some insects; also, petals of fruit-tree blossoms.
NEST Often incorporates string, yarn and plant fibers; built 15 ft above ground on horizontal limbs.
EGGS 4–5 elongated eggs; gray with brown spots.

This is an elegant bird in both form and color. Its chest and head are brown, blending seamlessly with the lemon-yellow belly. A black eye-stripe and tapered crest mark the head, and the tail tip has a band of brilliant yellow – a waxwing exclusive. The "wax" referred to in the name is actually the tips of the secondary wing feather quills, which form bright scarlet teardrops; oddly, not every waxwing has these specialized quills.

Humans without excellent hearing may miss the call of the cedar waxwing, a very high, trilled whistle that it gives out incessantly, especially in flight. Waxwings are gregarious birds, and have been known to nest in loose colonies, generally sticking to fairly open country with an abundance of large trees. The nest, which often incorporates string, yarn and plant fibers, is built about 15 feet above the ground on a horizontal limb.

The four or five young start out on an insect diet, but within days the parents begin to switch the chicks over to berries, which are regurgitated by the adults. The food literally goes in one end and comes out the other – in one study it took a young waxwing only 16 minutes, on average, to process each serving.

Almost any fruiting tree or shrub will attract waxwings to a yard; mountain ash, pyracantha, chokecherries, mulberries and cotoneasters work especially well. Waxwings also have the odd habit of eating the petals of fruit tree blossoms, in particular those of apple trees.

Cedar waxwings are found in a wide band across the middle latitudes of North America. Some stay in one area year-round, but others migrate to the southern U.S., Mexico and South America.

EUROPEAN STARLING
STURNUS VULGARIS

It is hard to find something nice to say about the starling; it is an aggressive bird with a penchant for stealing the nest cavities of native species and a talent for hogging feeders. Even its song has all the charm of a squeaking wheel. Still, one can at least be complimentary about its durability: the starling is one of the most successful birds in North America. It is found in every corner of the continent, in almost every imaginable habitat. Even more remarkably, it achieved this in less than a century.

In 1890, 60 starlings were released in New York City by a group that wanted to introduce all the birds mentioned in the works of Shakespeare. That they succeeded beyond their wildest dreams – at least with the starling – can be appreciated by witnessing these black birds cramming by the millions into nighttime roosts in the fall.

As might be expected of a bird so widespread, the starling is not picky about habitat or food. It avoids deep woods, preferring to stick to agricultural and urban areas, where it scavenges for insects, grain, seeds, fruit and berries (not to mention bird feeder handouts and even the dog food from Fido's dish). It is a cavity nester, and since it does not excavate its own hole, it relies on those of other birds – and if the hole is already occupied, the starling will simply harass the original owner until it takes possession.

DISTRIBUTION AND IDENTIFICATION

PLUMAGE Black (with purple-green sheen in spring; duller, with liberal white spotting in winter); short tail. Immatures brownish-gray.

HABITAT Very widespread in agricultural and urban areas.

FOOD Insects, grain, seeds, fruits and berries; also bird-feeders.

NEST In cavities built by other birds.

EGGS 4–6 eggs; very pale blue-green.

In flight and at rest, a starling has a plump, short-tailed profile. In spring, the adults' black feathers have a glossy, purple-green sheen. The winter plumage, acquired in the fall, is duller, with hundreds of white spots. Immatures are brownish-gray, with brown beaks.

RED-EYED VIREO
VIREO OLIVACEUS

In all but the West Coast and desert Southwest, the red-eyed vireo is a common forest bird, sticking to the canopy layer – the high treetops.

For that reason, this vireo can be difficult to see, despite its abundance. But where eyes fail, the ears will serve, because the red-eye is a tireless singer. Sometimes for hours on end, a male will whistle his ever-changing series of short phrases. Because of the song's fancied similarity to a non-stop sermon, the vireo was known as the "preacher bird" for many years.

DISTRIBUTION AND IDENTIFICATION

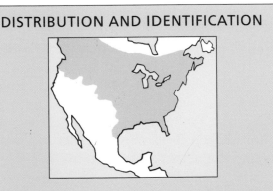

PLUMAGE Pale cream belly and greenish-brown back. Gray cap; white eye-stripe edged with black.
HABITAT In forests' high treetops; also in shady town streets, parks and residential areas with tall deciduous trees.
FOOD Insects.
NEST Artfully woven in the fork of a small branch; covered with outer layer of spider silk and lichen; built close to ground.
EGGS 3–4 white eggs, spotted with brown at large end.

The sexes among all of North America's 11 vireo species are identical. The red-eye, one of the most widespread species, is six inches long, with a pale cream belly, greenish-brown back, gray cap and a white eye-stripe edged with black. The red eye makes a poor field mark, because it is visible only when the bird is at very close range.

Vireos greatly resemble warblers, but are distinguished by their heavy, slightly hooked beaks. Like warblers, however, they are insectivorous, and share many of the same habitats.

Red-eyed vireos are most common in deciduous woods, including shady town streets, parks and residential neighborhoods with lots of tall trees and rich undergrowth. Even though it forages in the highest branches of the highest trees, red-eyed vireos nest much closer to the ground, often in a sapling only 20 or 30 feet high. The nest is artfully built in the fork of a small branch, woven so that it is suspended between the two forks. Covered as it is with an outer layer of spider silk and lichen, the nest resembles a much larger version of a ruby-throated hummingbird's. The eggs are white, with a circle of fine dark spots around the larger end – "wreathing," in the lexicon of the old egg-collectors.

The red-eyed vireo is one of the species most heavily parasitized by brown-headed cowbirds. Because cowbirds rarely venture far into unbroken forests, the fragmentation of a large area of woodland – for logging, houses or agriculture – usually means an increase in cowbirds and a decrease in vireos and other forest-nesting songbirds.

WARBLING VIREO
VIREO GILVUS

Birders use lots of verbal mnemonics to help them remember bird songs, usually by translating the song's rhythm and phrasing into a (frequently ridiculous) English equivalent. Thus, the warbling's vireo's rambling song becomes: *"When I sees one I shall seize one and I'll squeeze it 'till it squirts!,"* with a rising emphasis on the final note.

Actually, by its song is the best way to identify this rather drab vireo, found in deciduous forests over most of the continent. A simple white eye-stripe is the only field mark on this otherwise gray-green bird.

Open woodlands, tree-lined suburban areas and stream valleys are the usual home of the warbling vireo. For breeding, it almost always picks a poplar, maple, elm, ash, willow or other large tree, building its nest at least 40 or 50 feet above the ground. The nest, attached to the fork of a branch in a manner

similar to a red-eyed vireo's, is a silky cup about three and a half inches wide, bound up with spiderwebs and lined with fine stems and animal hair.

As with many birds that have ranges thousands of miles wide, warbling vireos from different areas show slight differences in coloration. Those from the East are the grayest, while western birds are a bit smaller, with a strong wash of yellow on their sides, particularly in fall. In the late 1800s, the western warbling vireo was considered a separate species, but more scientific thinking has since prevailed, and it is now thought to be nothing more than a geographic variation.

DISTRIBUTION AND IDENTIFICATION

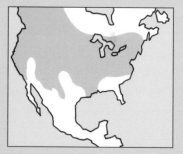

PLUMAGE Drab gray-green, with white eye-stripe.

HABITAT Open woodlands, tree-lined suburbs and stream valleys.

FOOD Insects.

NEST Silky cups bound with spiderwebs and lined with fine stems and animal hair; in large trees, 40–50 ft above ground.

EGGS 3–4 eggs; white with a few dark spots at the large end.

PROTHONOTARY WARBLER
PROTONOTARIA CITREA

Aldo Leopold, the great naturalist, once wrote that the prothonotary warbler was "the real jewel of my disease-ridden woodlot" – both a compliment to this bird's undisputed beauty, and a reference to its habit of nesting in the nooks and crannies of old, virus- and insect-smitten trees.

Leopold realized what many people still do not – that dead and dying trees are often as valuable to wildlife as healthy, growing specimens. A dead tree supports carpenter ants, wood-boring beetles and dozens of other insects. The woodpeckers that hunt for the bugs create holes that other birds need for nesting. Heart rot and similar tree diseases perform much the same task, opening up natural cavities used by birds, raccoons, squirrels and a host of other creatures. A dead tree goes on "living" long after the leaves finally wither.

DISTRIBUTION AND IDENTIFICATION

PLUMAGE Male: gold on head and underparts, with olive back and blue-gray wings and tail. Female: duller, with olive cast to head.

HABITAT Wooded swamps, moist bottomlands, some coastal areas.

FOOD Insects.

NEST In old, dead trees, preferably over water; lined with moss, leaves and grass.

EGGS 4–6 creamy eggs with brown blotches.

The prothonotary is a wood warbler, the second largest group of North American songbirds. Warblers are small, brightly colored (with a few exceptions) and highly migratory insect-eaters. The prothonotary, for example, migrates from Central and South America, returning each spring to the wooded swamps and moist bottomlands of the South and Midwest. It ranges farther north along the East Coast, and along the Mississippi drainage.

Males are an intense gold on the head and underparts, with an olive back and blue-gray wings and tail; the female is a duller version of the same, with an olive cast to her head. The male's song, four or five loud *tsweet, tsweet, tsweet, tsweet* notes, is often heard in the stifling heat of midday.

As part of his courtship ritual, the male prothonotary will build "dummy" nests, but once he has secured a mate, she builds the nest that will actually be used. Whenever possible, this species chooses a cavity over water, perhaps to discourage predators. The hole is lined – sometimes to great depth – with moss, leaves and grass.

BLUE-WINGED WARBLER

VERMIVORA PINUS

From the top of an aspen sapling in an overgrown meadow, a male blue-winged warbler sings his two-part song, *bee-bzzzzzzzzzzz*, the second part lower and convincingly insect like.

The warbler itself is yellow, with a black eye-stripe, blue-gray wings and white wingbars. It is an active bird, very visible as it flits from singing perch to singing perch, or hovers among the waving branches of a tree to catch insects.

Blue-winged warblers range from Alabama north through the Midwest and into southern New England, most often found where fields have reverted to brush and trees.

It is rapidly expanding its range to the Northeast, and as it moves into a new area, birders have noticed that the golden-winged warbler, a closely related species that shares the same habitat, usually disappears. It may be that the blue-winged is more aggressive and drives the golden-winged species away, or it could be that the habitat has changed, in ways we don't fully understand, to favor one species over the other.

The replacement of blue-winged for golden-winged does not take place overnight and where the two species breed in the same area they frequently hybridize. For many years, the two distinct hybrids – "Lawrence's" and "Brewster's" warblers – were

DISTRIBUTION AND IDENTIFICATION

PLUMAGE Yellow, with black eye-stripe. Blue-gray wings and white wingbars.

HABITAT Mostly in fields which have reverted to brush and trees.

FOOD Insects.

NEST A cup of grass and grapevine bark on the ground, under the shade of a weed clump or low bush in an overgrown meadow.

EGGS 4–6 white eggs with fine brown spots.

thought to be separate species.

The blue-winged warbler nests on the ground, constructing a cup of grass and grapevine bark under the shade of a weed clump or low bush in an overgrown meadow. The four or five eggs are white, speckled with fine brown spots.

ORANGE-CROWNED WARBLER
VERMIVORA CELATA

It's there, but don't expect to spot the patch of rusty brown on the head of the orange-crowned warbler without trying. This bird is common in the brushy woodlands and old meadows of the West and is also found across much of Canada, as far east as Labrador, but is a much rarer find there.

Five inches long and sooty olive, the orange-crowned's only field marks are faint streaks on the breast, a pale olive eye-stripe and yellow undertail feathers, but even experts sometimes have trouble identifying this dingy bird. To further complicate matters, there are three subspecies, each with slightly different colors: the western form is brightest yellow underneath, while the birds become progressively drabber the farther east they are found.

However difficult identification may be for people, the warblers themselves have no problems. The male's song – a high trill followed by a lower trill – instantly distinguishes him to female orange-crowneds. Depending on the area, the nest may be on the ground, or in a low bush.

The orange-crowned warbler is insectivorous in the summer, but is known to feed on berries and small fruits, especially in the fall and winter. Instead of migrating to the Tropics, as most warblers do, this bird retreats to the U.S.-Mexico border and to the Gulf States. On its wintering grounds, it can be lured to a feeder with suet or a mixture of peanut butter and rolled oats.

During the fall migration, the orange-crowned crosses North America on a northwest-to-southeast path. Even though it winters across a wide area of the South, it is a rare migrant in the East, occasionally spotted in small, mixed flocks of other warblers. Unfortunately for bird-watchers, it is so nondescript that most are simply passed over by observers who don't realize they are looking at a rarity.

DISTRIBUTION AND IDENTIFICATION

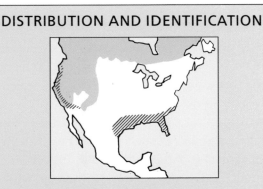

PLUMAGE Sooty olive, with faint breast streaks, pale olive eye-stripe and yellow undertail feathers. Patch of rusty brown on head.

HABITAT Brushy woodlands and old meadows.

FOOD Insects in summer, berries and small fruits in winter; come to feeder.

NEST Built on or near ground, made of grasses, leaves and bark shreds.

EGGS 4–5 white eggs with brown or gray spotting.

BLACK-AND-WHITE WARBLER
MNIOTILTA VARIA

This is the warbler that seems to think it is a nuthatch, creeping up and down tree trunks. Although it does not have a nuthatch's strongly clawed feet, or a woodpecker's brace-like tail, it has developed a longer, more curved bill, for probing in the corrugations of tree bark.

The black-and-white warbler is a good example of how all living things adapt to a "niche"; that is, how each species finds a habitat and lifestyle that it fully exploits. By carefully scouring the bark and branches of trees, the black-and-white warbler avoids competing with other species that hunt for flying insects, or that search through treetop leaves for food.

This warbler's name explains its coloration concisely – white, with black wings and tail, and heavy streaking on the head and sides. The male also has a black throat, which is white in the female. Its song is a thin *wee-see wee-see wee-see*, repeated a half-dozen times.

DISTRIBUTION AND IDENTIFICATION

PLUMAGE White, with black wings and tail; heavy streaking on head and sides. Male has black throat, female white.

HABITAT Deciduous forests.

FOOD Insects; some berries in early spring.

NEST Outer shell of weathered leaves, with bark, grass and rootlets woven to make the cup; on the ground at the base of a tree or against a rock, stump, log.

EGGS 4–5 eggs; white with brown wreathing and spotting.

The black-and-white is found across almost all of the East and into central Canada. It is one of the earliest warblers to return in the spring, often arriving well before the oaks and maples have leafed out, and usually weeks ahead of most other species.

The nest is built on the ground at the base of a tree, or tight against a large rock, stump or log. Weathered leaves form the outer shell of the nest, with bark, grass and rootlets woven to make the cup. When the chicks are old enough to move, they often scramble into the branches of saplings and bushes, thus making themselves a little less vulnerable to attacks from weasels, snakes and other ground-hunting predators.

BLACKBURNIAN WARBLER
DENDROICA FUSCA

DISTRIBUTION AND IDENTIFICATION

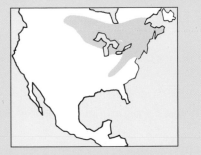

PLUMAGE Male: orange face, with black and white accents. Female: same basic pattern, but without brilliant orange and deep black.

HABITAT Deep, moist coniferous forests; in parks, backyards, any wooded areas in spring and fall.

FOOD Insects.

NEST Built high up a tree, usually a spruce; lined with *Usnea*, a mossy lichen.

EGGS 4–5 off-white eggs, wreathed and spotted in brown.

The spring warbler migration is a high point in any bird-watcher's year. The flocks, after flying all night, spill out of the dawn air to feed frantically. At times, the trees seem alive with birds, all colored like the rainbow.

But even in this chaotic scene of movement and color, one bird stands out – the male blackburnian warbler, with his vividly orange face, accented with black and white.

The blackburnian likes deep, moist forests of conifers for nesting, and so has a fairly restricted breeding range – up the higher ridges of the Appalachians, through New England, the Great Lakes region and southern Canada. To find it during the summer, one must look to the mountaintops, but during the spring and fall migrations it, like so many other songbirds, may be found in parks, backyards and in almost any wooded area.

The nest is built very high up, usually in a spruce, and is almost always lined with *Usnea*, a mossy lichen that grows in droopy clumps from the branches of spruce trees. The blackburnian's fondness for *Usnea* poses a problem, because the lichen is disappearing in many locations, possibly a victim of air pollution. It is not yet known if this will have an effect on the warbler, but it points up the inter-relatedness of all living things, even those that seem unconnected.

The female blackburnian has the same basic pattern as her mate, but has none of the brilliant orange or deep black tones. Many of the early ornithologists were understandably confused by the different plumages of male, female and immature warblers. The female blackburnian, for example, was for many years believed to be a different bird entirely, and was called the hemlock warbler.

CHESTNUT-SIDED WARBLER
DENDROICA PENSYLVANICA

DISTRIBUTION AND IDENTIFICATION

PLUMAGE Male: strip of chestnut running down sides and bright yellow cap. Female more subdued, with less chestnut; a dull yellow crown.

HABITAT Brushy fields, shrubby roadsides, young forests.

FOOD Insects.

NEST In low briars and bushes, sometimes including the sticky silk of the eastern tent caterpillar.

EGGS 3–4 off-white eggs with brown or purplish scrawlings.

Another specialty of the Northeast, the chestnut-sided warbler is a common bird of brushy fields, shrubby roadsides, old orchards and young, second-growth forests – in other words, much of the region. Such was not always the case. In Audubon's day it was so rare that he saw only one, an experience shared with other naturalists of the late 18th and early 19th centuries.

The male has a strip of chestnut running down each side, and a bright yellow cap. The female's pattern is a more subdued version of the male's, with lesser amounts of chestnut and a dull yellow crown. It is an active bird, bustling through the underbrush with its wings drooping and its tail cocked up at an angle.

The chestnut-sided is found from southern Canada, the upper Midwest and New England, down along the Appalachians. Oddly, it is also found breeding in a small area of central Colorado – the result, perhaps, of a storm during migration that blew a flock off-course. Migrating birds frequently go astray, and if their new home offers the right mix of food, habitat and climate, they sometimes survive, as appears to have been the case in Colorado.

Low briars and bushes are chosen to hold the nest, which the female builds by herself in about five days, sometimes using the sticky silk of the eastern tent caterpillar in the process.

The male's song is loud and brash, and is usually transcribed as *please please pleased ta meetcha*. He also has a second melody, longer and not as loud, that he sings during the two weeks the female is incubating their eggs.

YELLOW-RUMPED WARBLER
DENDROICA CORONATA

What's in a name? Once, the eastern race of this species was known as both the "yellow-crowned wood warbler," an accurate label reflecting its color and family, and the "yellow-rumped warbler," a less useful name in that many other warblers have yellow rumps. To eliminate the confusion, science settled on "myrtle warbler" as the common name (from the bird's habit of eating wax-myrtle berries in the fall), and that's where the matter stood for many years.

In the 1970s, however, biologists noticed that the myrtle warbler and a very similar western species, Audubon's warbler, freely hybridized – suggesting that they weren't true, distinct species, but rather merely geographic forms. The result: the two were lumped together as one in the eyes of ornithology, and the old/new name yellow-rumped warbler was applied to both.

The eastern and western forms look very much alike – dark blue-gray wings and head, a yellow rump patch, crown and sides, and a dark band across the breast. The only real difference is the throat, white in the east and yellow in the west. In flight, or when agitated, the yellow-rumped flashes its tail feathers, showing bold white marks on either side. Females are somewhat duller, especially in fall.

Yellow-rumpeds are common in coniferous or mixed forests across most of Canada, New England and the West. They nest 20 or 30 feet above the ground, in the branches of conifers. The nest, built of

twigs and bark, is almost always lined with feathers, which the female weaves into the cup in such a way that they curve over the eggs, hiding them when the female is off the nest.

This species winters farther north than any other warbler, frequently braving the winters of Washington, Oregon and New England. Foraging in small flocks, it stays in thick cover with plenty of poison ivy, greenbrier and Virginia creeper berries, often where conifer plantings provide some protection from the cold wind. Along the coast, bayberries and red cedar berries are staple foods.

DISTRIBUTION AND IDENTIFICATION

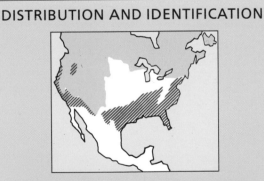

PLUMAGE Dark blue-gray wings and head; dark band across breast. Yellow rump patch, crown and sides. Bold white marks on tail in flight. White throat in eastern form; yellow in western.
HABITAT Coniferous or mixed forests.
FOOD Insects and berries.
NEST Of twigs and bark, lined with feathers woven into the cup to curve over eggs; in branches of conifers 20 or so ft up.
EGGS 4–5 eggs; white with brown wreathing at large end.

BLACK-THROATED GRAY WARBLER
DENDROICA NIGRESCENS

DISTRIBUTION AND IDENTIFICATION

PLUMAGE Deep, slaty blue, with black head markings and black throat. Fleck of gold in front of eye.

HABITAT Warm, dry forests of oak, pinyon and manzanita bushes.

FOOD Insects.

NEST Compact cup of leaves, fuzzy bark shreds and plant down, secured together with spider silk and lined with feathers; 20–30 ft up, well out from the tree trunk.

EGGS 3–5 white eggs with sparse brown wreathing.

The black-throated gray warbler is proof that a bird need not be colorful to be attractive. Both sexes are deep, slaty blue, with black head markings. The only color is a tiny fleck of gold in front of the eye – an accent that sets off the rest of the bird's austere pattern nicely.

The black-throated gray is restricted to warm, dry forests of oak, pinyon and manzanita bushes, from New Mexico northwest to British Columbia. Within the proper habitat it is fairly common, singing a buzzy *weezy weezy weezy weezy-weet*. Except when the male sings, however, it is a quiet, retiring species that stays mostly out of sight.

Its nest is generally built about 20 or 30 feet above the ground, and well out from the trunk of the tree. The compact cup is made of leaves, fuzzy bark shreds and plant down, secured together (and to the branch) with spider silk. The lining is almost always feathers, although they are not so carefully arranged as in the yellow-rumped warbler's nest.

YELLOW WARBLER
DENDROICA PETECHIA

such situations that also have a stream or pond nearby. But rather than sulking in some hidden nook, as so many warblers do, the yellow warbler stays in the open, singing from the top of the tallest trees – *sweet sweet sweet I'm so sweet* – or darting like a sunbeam through the foliage.

The nest, in the crotch of a sapling or bush, looks less like a bird's nest than it does a ball of lint, for the yellow warbler has a fondness for soft, fuzzy building materials, including plant down, hair, old string, milkweed fibers and grass. The warbler lays four or five eggs – average for its family – that are white with brown or gray wreathing.

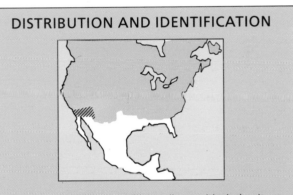

DISTRIBUTION AND IDENTIFICATION

PLUMAGE Male: deep golden yellow, with dark wings and chestnut breast streaking. Female: lighter yellow, fading to gray on head and back.
HABITAT Areas of dense plant growth (old orchards, roadside hedges, etc.) near streams and ponds.
FOOD Insects.
NEST Of soft, fuzzy materials such as plant down, hair, old string, grass; in crotches of saplings or bushes.
EGGS 4–5 pale bluish eggs with brown splotches and wreathing.

Except for Texas and the Deep South, all of North America enjoys the bell-clear song of the yellow warbler, one of the most widespread songbirds on the continent – and one of the most beautiful. The male is a deep, golden yellow, with dark wings and bright, chestnut streaking on his breast. The female is a quieter shade of yellow, fading to gray on the head and back.

Willow thickets, alder-choked stream banks, old orchards, roadside hedges, meadows reverting to woodland – these are the haunts of this species, where the plant growth is a riot of young saplings and dense brush. They are especially common in

The yellow warbler is a perennial victim of the brown-headed cowbird. The cowbird eggs are usually incubated and the chicks raised, but like the eastern phoebe, the yellow warbler sometimes thwarts the cowbird by building additional layers to its nest, even if it means abandoning some of its own eggs in the process.

OVENBIRD
SEIURUS AUROCAPILLUS

The ovenbird makes no secret of its presence. From late April through mid-summer, the males proclaim their territories with a vigor – and volume – uncommon in most small birds. The song is a ringing *tea-chur tea-CHUR TEA-CHUR TEA-CHUR*, building in insistence and rising in tone toward the end.

The song of the ovenbird is one of the most familiar sounds of the eastern woods, partly because it is so loud, in part because the ovenbird is so common. It is found from the southern mountains into Canada, and northwest to British Columbia in a rather spotty distribution. The ovenbird prefers maturing forests of deciduous trees, woods that have grown past the

DISTRIBUTION AND IDENTIFICATION

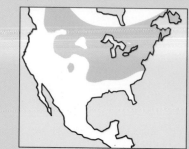

PLUMAGE Olive-brown back and head; white breast with black streaks. Black-edged crown of rusty brown.

HABITAT On the floor of maturing forests of deciduous trees.

FOOD Insects.

NEST Cup hidden in a small hollow, with a half-roof of leaves overhead; built on ground amid dead leaves.

EGGS 3–5 eggs; white with reddish-brown spots and wreathing.

sapling stage and which have a fairly clear understory, clean of shrubs. In this park-like setting, the ovenbird male chooses a horizontal or diagonal branch, near the ground, as his singing post.

It is much harder to see an ovenbird than to hear one. The singing males stay fairly still, and the bird's color blends well with the surroundings. Sexes are identical – an olive-brown back and head, white breast with black streaks, and a black-edged crown of rusty brown. This species, a warbler, spends much of its time on the forest floor hunting insects, moving with a deliberate walk.

The ovenbird's name comes from its unusual nest, built on the ground amid dead leaves. The cup is hidden in a small hollow, with a half-roof of leaves overhead like an old-fashioned bake oven. The female enters from the side, only after alighting quite a distance away and sneaking in, to fool predators.

COMMON YELLOWTHROAT
GEOTHLYPIS TRICHAS

An abundant, widespread warbler, the common yellowthroat is a bantam-weight fighter, a tiny bird with the nerve to take on any opponent that enters its territory.

Hawk or human, the reaction is the same. The male yellowthroat, spoiling for an argument, bounces from one perch to another, his short tail angled high and his head held low, scolding with emphatic *tcheck* notes. Kissing on the back of one's hand to make a squeaking sound only infuriates him more, usually bringing him into full view. About five inches long, he has a black mask, bright yellow throat and greenish back, wings and tail. His mate, who will probably hang farther back in the thicket, lacks the mask.

Yellowthroats are common birds wherever man has cleared the forest and allowed thick cover to spring up. They are especially fond of wet areas, like alder tangles along the verge of streams, or moist meadows where sedges, young willows and wild roses grow in profusion. This species is found continent-wide, from the Mexican border to the Yukon.

The yellowthroat's song is a rolling *witchity witchity witchity witchity witchity* in most areas, but there is a good deal of variation between different regions. There are slight differences, as well, in color among various areas of North America, and as many as 12 subspecies have been cataloged.

The female yellowthroat handles the nest-building chores, weaving strands of grass blades and weed leaves into a cup that is hidden deep within thick grass, often in the shade of a bush. For as belligerent as it can be elsewhere in its territory, a yellowthroat is quite secretive around its nest, coming and going without any fanfare.

DISTRIBUTION AND IDENTIFICATION

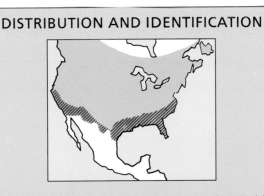

PLUMAGE Black mask, yellow throat and greenish back, wings and short tail. Female lacks the mask.

HABITAT Cleared forests of thick cover, especially wet areas.

FOOD Insects.

NEST Strands of grass blades and weed leaves woven into a cup hidden deep within thick grass.

EGGS 4–5 white eggs with dark speckles and wreathing.

YELLOW-BREASTED CHAT
ICTERIA VIRENS

DISTRIBUTION AND IDENTIFICATION

PLUMAGE Yellow chest and throat, gray-green back, and dark head. White "spectacles" around eyes. Long tail.

HABITAT Brushy meadows, orchards and fencerows.

FOOD Insects, spiders, fruit and berries.

NEST Large structure of straw, grass, leaves and weed stems, usually in a low blackberry bush or like tangle.

EGGS 4 or 5 eggs; white with heavy brown spotting.

With its large size and long tail, the chat looks more akin to the thrashers, but it is a warbler – at seven and a half inches, easily the largest of that clan.

Like the yellowthroat, which it somewhat resembles, the yellow-breasted chat is a summer resident of brushy meadows, orchards and fencerows; its range encompasses almost all the United States, but does not extend into Canada.

The chat's yellow chest and throat are its major field marks, coupled with a gray-green back, tail and dark head, with white "spectacles" around each eye. Equally distinctive is the chat's disjointed way of flying, as if its wings, tail and feet were hanging on by the barest thread, and might at any moment fall completely apart. The male has a unique courtship flight, during which he climbs almost vertically into the air, flapping deeply with his feet drooping down, all the while singing a medley of gurgles and whistles.

At other times, his vocalizations are less musical. Some individuals are accomplished mimics, but the talent is by no means universal, and the normal call is a jumble of short phrases, given in no particular order. The diversity of sounds that a chat creates may, in part, account for its reputation as a mimic; listen long enough, and one is sure to hear a note that resembles *something* else.

A chat's nest is usually built in a low blackberry bush or similar tangle, with straw, grass, leaves and weed stems making up the relatively large structure. Insects, spiders, fruit and berries are eaten by both the adults and chicks.

Along the northern edge of its range, the yellow-breasted chat has experienced some fairly serious declines, especially in the Northeast. Outwardly there would seem to be little reason for the decrease, since the habitat chats favor is hardly scarce. But there is more to habitat than meets the eye, and the chats apparently have suffered from some lack that we are not yet aware of.

ROSE-BREASTED GROSBEAK
PHEUCTICUS LUDOVICIANUS

Beautiful in appearance and in voice, the male rose-breasted grosbeak is at his loveliest in a shaft of sunlight, with the green shadows of the forest to counterpoint his red breast and white belly.

The rose-breasted is a finch, related to the sparrows, and reaches a length of between seven and eight inches. The male is boldly marked, with a black head, throat, back and wings, white undersides and a triangle of rosy-red in the center of his breast. In flight, he shows large patches of white on his wings and rump, as well as red wing linings. The female, on the other hand, is basically brown, with a buffy, streaked breast, a white eyeline and no red. Young males, frequently seen in the fall, look like females, but with a pink wash over the breast.

Deciduous forests over the northeastern third of the continent are home to the rose-breasted, from Kansas and the Appalachians through New England and central Canada. It is found most often at the edge of the forest, where the trees abut a meadow, marsh, lake or yard.

The song of a rose-breasted grosbeak is similar in phrasing to a robin's, but with a clearer tone and faster pace. Males often sing while flying after females, giving the impression of a failed suitor that just won't quit. Among most songbirds only the males sing, but female rose-breasteds have a song of their own as well, usually sung on the nest.

A glance at its heavy bill – the "gross," or large, beak of its name – might suggest that this species subsists on thick-hulled seeds, but in truth it feeds on insects, fruits and berries. A plentiful food supply, prime singing perches and good nest sites are all requirements when the male sets up his territory; for the latter, a forked tree branch about 15 feet off the ground is chosen. The nest cup is poorly made, but the eggs themselves are very attractive – pale bluish-green, heavily speckled with brown and wreathed at the large end.

A summer feeding station that offers sunflower seeds and pieces of diced fruit will sometimes lure a family of grosbeaks; the sight of four or five fledglings lined up for chow, with both parents in attendance, is enough to make the off-season effort worthwhile.

DISTRIBUTION AND IDENTIFICATION

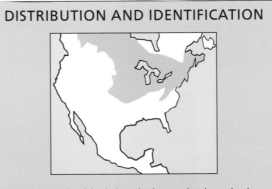

PLUMAGE Male: black head, throat, back and wings, white undersides and a triangle of rosy-red in center of breast. Female: mostly brown, with buffy streaked breast, white eyeline and no red. (Young male like female, but with pink wash over breast.)
HABITAT Mostly at edges of deciduous forests near meadows, marshes or lakes, over northeastern third of North America.
FOOD Insects, fruits and berries.
NEST A poory made cup, in forked tree branches 15 ft up.
EGGS 4–5 glossy, bluish eggs, heavily spotted with brown and wreathed at large end.

BLACK-HEADED GROSBEAK
PHEUCTICUS MELANOCEPHALUS

The western equivalent of the rose-breasted grosbeak is the black-headed grosbeak – in fact, the two species hybridize where their ranges overlap in the Plains.

In many ways, the life histories of the rose-breasted and black-headed grosbeaks mirror each other. As the rose-breasted is found in fairly open deciduous forests, so is this western species most commonly seen in groves of oaks, aspens and alders, especially in moist woodlands near water. The eggs of the two species are indistinguishable, and both build fairly primitive nests in low trees and shrubs. Even their songs and *eek* alarm notes are almost identical.

Yet, despite such similarity of lifestyle, there is no confusing a male black-headed grosbeak with his eastern cousin. A shade over eight inches long, he has the large head and heavy beak that mark the grosbeaks, but his throat, breast and rump are rusty orange, a color that extends as well in a partial collar around his neck. The female, on the other hand, looks confusingly like an immature male rose-breasted, differentiated largely by her yellow, rather than pink, wing linings.

Before Europeans settled in North America, the black-headed and rose-breasted grosbeaks – both forest birds – were separated by the treeless expanse of the Great Plains. But with the coming of the white man, shelter belts, parks, fencelines and wooded yards sprang up across the prairie, creating forested

DISTRIBUTION AND IDENTIFICATION

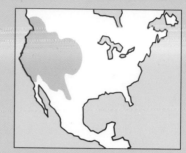

PLUMAGE Male: rusty orange throat, breast and rump; black head. Female: basically brown, with pink wash over breast and yellow wing linings.

HABITAT In groves of oaks, aspens and alders, especially in moist woodlands near water.

FOOD Insects, fruits and berries.

NEST Primitive nest in low trees and shrubs.

EGGS 4–5 glossy, bluish eggs, heavily spotted with brown and wreathed at large end.

habitat where none existed before. The rose-breasted grosbeak moved west, and to a lesser degree the black-headed expanded east. The two species, kept apart for so long, met and cross-bred; the first hybrids were discovered in the early 1920s in Nebraska, and are now rather commonplace. Some scientists have suggested coining the term *semi-species* to describe birds, like these, that interbreed so freely where their ranges overlap.

NORTHERN CARDINAL
CARDINALIS CARDINALIS

Easily one of the best-loved and best-known birds in North America, the cardinal is unmistakable, with its fire-engine-red color and jaunty crest. Even more endearing is the fact that the cardinal is one of the most common feeder birds, cracking sunflower seed hulls with its powerful beak.

Cardinals are birds of the forest edge, where brushy thickets provide protection. For that reason, they adapt easily to suburbia, with its backyard plantings of shrubs and shade trees. Here, in spring, the males stake out territories, singing *cheer cheer cheer, whoit whoit whoit whoit* to the mild morning. Interestingly, the cardinal is, like the rose-breasted grosbeak, one of the few species in which the female sings with a skill equal to the male, although their songs appear to play less of a role in territorial defense.

Male cardinals, with their brilliant color, get most of the attention, but the female is lovely as well, in a more subdued way. Her wings, tail and crest have just a touch of red, while her body feathers are a soft blend of buff and pink.

The cardinal ranges across the South and East, from southern Arizona to Florida and north to Minnesota, southern Ontario and New England; the species has, like the mockingbird, dramatically expanded its range to the north in recent decades.

The nest is generally built in low bushes, hedges or small, shrubby trees. In most cases the pair will be very defensive of its territory – the males chasing other males, the females pursuing encroaching females. Sometimes those barriers break down, however, and two females have been known to share the same nest, splitting incubation duties.

DISTRIBUTION AND IDENTIFICATION

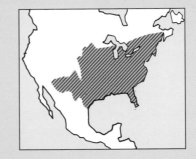

PLUMAGE Male: fire-engine red with jaunty crest. Female's wings, tail and crest have touch of red; body a soft blend of buff and pink.

HABITAT At forest edges, but adapt to suburbia with backyard shrubs and shade trees.

FOOD Seeds, fruits, small nuts; insects in summer; common bird-feeder.

NEST Cup of grass, twigs and leaves, often lined with hair; built in low bushes, hedges or small shrubby trees.

EGGS 3–4 eggs; off-white with heavy brown or purplish markings.

BLUE GROSBEAK
GUIRACA CAERULEA

Songbirds do not like snakes, and often with good reason. Blacksnakes and other species are major predators on those birds that nest on the ground and in low bushes, and even birds that place their nests 20 or more feet up are not immune from attack. So it is an open question why several birds include shed snakeskins in their nests – among them the blue grosbeak, which (like the great crested flycatcher and tufted titmouse) makes a habit of it. Originally it was believed that the skins were placed around the nest to scare away meat-eaters, but research has shown that predators are not in the least frightened of empty snakeskins. It is more likely that the tissue-thin skins are simply an attractive building material (they have been found in the nests of more than 30 bird species), and that a few varieties have made a practice out of using them, as other birds habitually use mud, or dead leaves.

The blue grosbeak is a confirmed Southerner, occurring in a wide belt from southern California to the Mid-Atlantic seaboard. Although it is pushing north along the coast, it remains a rarity above the Mason-Dixon line.

The blue grosbeak is commonly confused with the much smaller indigo bunting, which occupies much the same habitat: brushy pastures, forest edges and yards. The male grosbeak's chestnut-colored wing-bars and very heavy bill are the best field marks for separating it from the all-blue bunting. Female blue grosbeaks are brown, with rusty wingbars and faintly blue shoulder pads. Both sexes have a habit of nervously flicking their tail – a handy characteristic that can identify this bird even at a distance.

DISTRIBUTION AND IDENTIFICATION

PLUMAGE Male: blue with chestnut wingbars. Female:
brown with rusty wingbars and faintly blue shoulder pads.

HABITAT Brushy pastures, forest edges and yards.

FOOD Insects, grains and weed seeds.

NEST Well-built cup of grass, leaves and stems; often includes snakeskins; built near ground in thick vegetation.

EGGS 4–5 white or pale blue eggs.

INDIGO BUNTING
PASSERINA CYANEA

The indigo bunting says everything twice – the male's song is a series of couplets, sung with gusto from the top of a roadside walnut tree, or the crown of a wild blackberry hedge.

More brilliantly blue than any of the bluebirds, the indigo bunting is an abundant summer resident over all of the East, and down into parts of the Southwest, where its range is growing. Sparrow-sized, with a much smaller bill than the blue grosbeak, the male is solid blue above and below. His mate is a drab brown, with virtually no identifying features

A cardinal's bright red feathers are colored that way because the feather fibers contain a red pigment, zoonerythrin, that makes the bird appear red even

DISTRIBUTION AND IDENTIFICATION

PLUMAGE Male: solid blue above and below. Female: drab brown.

HABITAT Brushy pastures, forest edges and yards.

FOOD Insects, weed seeds.

NEST Grass and weed leaves woven among stems of bushes, young trees or blackberry canes.

EGGS 3–5 white or pale blue eggs.

under poor lighting conditions. But blue-tinted birds, like the indigo bunting, are different. Their colors, like those of the hummingbird, are the result of feather structure.

In truth, the fibers of a bunting's feathers are dark brown – but each tiny barb is covered with a layer of special cells that breaks sunlight into the spectrum, then scatters everything but blue light. Thus, an indigo bunting in the sun glows with the richest blue imaginable, but the same bird can appear black if the angle of the light is wrong.

The female builds the nest herself, weaving grass and weed leaves among the supporting stems of bushes, young trees or blackberry canes. No matter the location, the nest is often found by brown-headed cowbirds, and such parasitism may be a major factor in limiting the bunting's population in some areas.

Through the nesting and chick-rearing period, the male continues to sing with almost obsessive fervor; one patient observer timed a bunting, which sang daily from 4 a.m. until 8 p.m., at a rate of six songs per minute – for a total of 4,320 songs per day!

PAINTED BUNTING
PASSERINA CIRIS

No other North American songbird exhibits such a clashing combination of colors as the male painted bunting – a red breast and rump, blue head, dark wings and lime-green back. The effect is, to say the least, striking.

The painted bunting's range encompasses much of the South, from Texas to South Carolina, but its distribution is spotty and it is at best only locally common.

Where it is found it is a frequent visitor to yards and stream borders, and in some areas is a common small-town bird.

A rather late migrant, the bunting returns from Central America in mid-April. Courtship involves a display by the male, who fans his feathers to show them off to greatest advantage. Nest-building and care of the young are almost completely the female's responsibility; it is she that builds the nest in a low bush or tangle, she that incubates and she that feeds the three or four chicks. Shortly after the young leave the nest, however, she may abandon them to the care of the heretofore uninvolved male, and go off to build a new nest for a second brood.

For his part, the male defends his territory with a ferocity rarely seen in songbirds. Most birds – most wild animals, for that matter – prefer to use ritual and bluff, rather than physical violence, to settle boundary disputes. Painted buntings, however, take part in bloody scraps that may end with the death of one of the combatants.

Painted buntings can be lured to bird feeders easily during the summer. Cracked corn and sunflower seeds will usually do the trick, especially if the feeding station is near escape cover and has water close at hand.

DISTRIBUTION AND IDENTIFICATION

PLUMAGE Male: red breast and rump; blue head, dark wings and lime-green black. Female: dark green above and yellowish below.

HABITAT Yards and stream borders, as well as small towns.

FOOD Seeds and insects; common feeder (cracked corn and sunflower seed).

NEST Deep cup of grass, built in low bushes or tangles.

EGGS 3–4 bluish-white eggs, spotted with brown.

RUFOUS-SIDED TOWHEE
PIPILO ERYTHROPHTHALMUS

Common over much of the U.S., the rufous-sided towhee has a classy look about it. An adult male has a black head, back and tail, white belly, rusty-orange side patches – and white wing – and tail bars; the female is patterned similarly, but is brown where the male is black. Western males have dozens of white spots on the back, which are absent in eastern birds.

The territorial song of the towhee is usually written as *Drink your te-e-a-a-a*, with the middle note lower than the rest and the final one a drawn-out trill. As the breeding season progresses, however (and as young males try their inexperienced voices), the songs become increasingly choppy, until by summer's end there are but a few towhees still singing, and then only partial songs: *Drink your . . .*, or sometimes just *te-e-a-a-a*.

Being a ground-feeder, it should not be surprising that the rufous-sided towhee is also a ground nester, either right on the forest floor or very low in surrounding shrubs. Sometimes the nest cup is built in a small hollow, so that the eggs are slightly below ground level.

DISTRIBUTION AND IDENTIFICATION

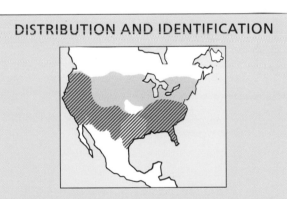

PLUMAGE Male: black head, back and tail; white belly, rusty-orange side patches, and white wings and tailbars. Female: brown where male is black. Western males also have dozens of white spots on their backs.

HABITAT Forests and thickets.

FOOD Insects, seeds, small nuts and berries.

NEST Cup built in small hollow on forest floor or low in surrounding shrubs.

EGGS 3–5 bone-white eggs, finely speckled with reddish-brown.

From a distance, it sounds like a deer crashing through the woods – a loud, almost continuous thrashing of leaves. But, as more than one hiker has discovered, the sound is as likely to come from an eight-inch bird as a 150-pound deer.

The rufous-sided towhee is a ground-feeder with flair, kicking both legs simultaneously as it rummages through the dead leaves that cover the forest floor. Periodically it will pause, cock a bright red eye at the woods for danger, and give one of its trademark calls, a clear, rising *cher-wink*. Then it will go back to the business of finding supper, making a racket in the process.

SONG SPARROW
MELOSPIZA MELODIA

The songs also vary on a region-to-region basis, but most follow a basic form: three or four clear, whistled notes, a buzzy phrase and finally a trill. Researchers analyzing recordings of their songs, and studying captive birds, have concluded that song sparrows are born with an instinctive ability to sing two kinds of songs, but that they can also modify their melodies by listening to others of the same species. Thus, all the songs in one area may have common elements that are missing from other regions. In a very real sense, these are dialects, just as in human speech.

The song sparrow likes its habitat brushy, although it isn't particular about what that brush is – wild grape and blackberry in Ohio, salt marshes in New England, tule beds in New Mexico and along ocean beaches in Alaska. The nest is usually built within 10 feet of the ground, filled with four or five pale eggs, very heavily spotted with reddish brown. It is second only to the yellow warbler as an unwitting host to cowbird chicks, which it raises, all unknowing, as its own.

*M*elospiza melodia – "song-finch with a pleasing song" – is this common bird's accurate, if tautological, scientific name. Found in almost every nook of North America, its sweet song is one of the most familiar sounds of springtime.

More than 30 subspecies have been recorded, each reflecting slight differences in size and color. The eastern form sets the standard for the species: both sexes have a long, rounded tail, brown streaky back, and a pale breast with fine streaks and a heavy, central spot. That spot, and heavy dark "whisker" marks along the throat, are the best field characteristics. As indicated, the song sparrow is highly variable; the desert race is quite pale, while song sparrows from Alaska's cold Aleutian Islands are much larger – a common adaptation to help conserve body heat.

DISTRIBUTION AND IDENTIFICATION

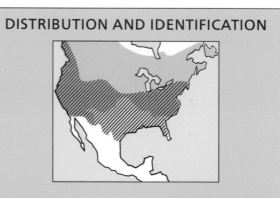

PLUMAGE Most of the species has brown streaky back, pale breast with fine streaks and heavy central spot; also heavy dark whisker marks along throat. Many variations throughout the continent.

HABITAT Brushy land in open country, city parks and gardens.

FOOD Insects and seeds.

NEST Small cup of grass and leaves on ground.

EGGS 4–5 eggs; greenish with very heavy red-brown speckling and splotching.

LARK SPARROW
CHONDESTES GRAMMACUS

DISTRIBUTION AND IDENTIFICATION

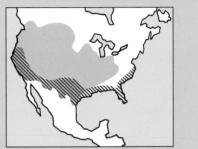

PLUMAGE Chestnut eyebrows and cheek patches with areas of white and black. Black tail shows large white corners and outer tail feathers in flight.

HABITAT Grasslands and prairies.

FOOD Insects (principally grasshoppers) and seeds.

NEST Grass-lined depression in ground, usually hidden by grasses or shrubs.

EGGS 4–5 off-white eggs with dark scrawls at large end.

Most sparrows are confusingly alike – all roughly the same size, told apart only by slight differences in streaking or spotting.

Not so the lark sparrow, one of the most attractive of North America's 31 sparrow species. A bird of the western grasslands, it has a distinctive facial pattern of chestnut eyebrows and cheek patches with areas of white and black – a most attractive combination. When it flies, the black tail shows large white corners and outer tail feathers. It is a hard bird to misidentify.

Among birds like lark sparrows, in which the sexes are identical, behavior usually replaces sight as the key to allowing the birds themselves to sort out which bird is what sex. When lark sparrows meet, the males go through a bill-pointing display, aiming their beak upward. A male responds in kind, and a fight may ensue. If the second bird is a female she will not respond – the signal for the male to go into his courtship display, which involves fanning his wings and singing.

As with many finches, the lark sparrow eats large quantities of insects (principally grasshoppers) and seeds. Where they are common, they feed in flocks, even during the breeding season, when most birds tend to be more solitary.

Once, the lark sparrow nested – albeit in small numbers – as far east as Pennsylvania and New York. In recent decades it has all but vanished from the eastern fringe of its range, and is now uncommon almost everywhere east of the Mississippi. Fortunately, it remains an abundant part of the bird life of the West, from the Canadian prairies to California and the Mexican border.

CHIPPING SPARROW
SPIZELLA PASSERINA

DISTRIBUTION AND IDENTIFICATION

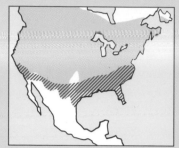

PLUMAGE Adults: rusty cap, white eyebrow and thin black eye-stripe. Pale gray breast; streaky brown back. Immatures: streaked brown crown, brown cheek patch and buffy breast.
HABITAT Backyards, fencerows and second-growth woodlands.
FOOD Insects and seeds.
NEST Grasses for outer shell, finer materials for inner; hair linings. Built in low, thick cover (small spruces, rose trellises etc.).
EGGS 4–5 eggs; blue-green with brown splotches.

Completely at home with people, the chipping sparrow is a familiar backyard bird in virtually all of the continent, with the exception only of the arctic and a tiny portion of the southern Plains.

Five inches long, the "chippy," as many know it, is the only sparrow to have a rusty cap, white eyebrow and thin, black eye-stripe. Its breast is pale gray; its back, streaky brown. In typical sparrow fashion, the sexes are identical.

Chipping sparrows have benefited greatly from the changes man has caused to the environment, especially in the East. Housing developments, fencerows and second-growth woodlands might be bad for wilderness species, but they provide the perfect habitat for this spritely bird.

Its song is a thin trill, machine-gun fast and on a single pitch. The male usually chooses a high, exposed perch from which to sing – a treetop, the peak of a house or a telephone wire.

Next to robins, chipping sparrows are the songbirds most likely to nest cheek-by-jowl with humans. The nest is built in whatever low, thick cover is available – small spruces or pines in the front yard, rose trellises, boxwood hedges or other bushes.

The female does all of the gathering and building, using grasses for the outer shell and working with progressively finer materials. For the lining, she will always use hair – horsehair, if it is available, or the long strands of dogs, raccoons, road-killed deer or cows.

One long-haired Boston woman, each morning after combing, would clean her hairbrush outside. Her reward was a chipping sparrow nest on the porch, thickly lined with blonde hair.

Immature chipping sparrows lack the adult's rusty cap and clean gray breast. Instead, they have a streaked, brown crown, brown cheek patch and buffy breast. They are a common sight in migration, and on the wintering grounds in the South.

DARK-EYED JUNCO
JUNCO HYEMALIS

The "snowbird" that comes south with winter at its heels, the dark-eyed junco is seen in many parts of North America only when the snow flies – but while the cold lasts, this gray sparrow will be one of the most common birds around.

The junco has several distinctive geographic races that were once broken into separate species. The "slate-colored" junco of the northern forest is the most widespread; it is uniformly gray, with a white belly that makes the bird look as though it sat in paint. The "Oregon" junco of the West has a black head, rusty back and sides, and dark wings, while the "gray-headed" junco of the southern Rockies and Southwest is gray top and bottom, with a chestnut back patch. In the South Dakota Black Hills is yet another form, the "white-winged" junco – superficially like the "slate-colored," but with white wing-bars. In flight, all the varieties display the major junco field mark – white outer tail feathers that flash when the bird flies.

With so many races, it might be best to concentrate on the "slate-colored," which is fairly representative of all. During the summer, the juncos stay in the forests, both in the North and along the Appalachians. At one time, the junco was considered a fairly rare breeder in much of its southerly range, but the advent of organized, statewide breeding bird censuses has changed that perception. In Pennsylvania, for example, the junco was found almost everywhere on the ridges that crisscross the state, and in New York, it was found wherever there were forests above 1,000 feet in elevation. Upturned tree roots, road banks and rocky slopes are the favored sites for the nest, which is built on the ground.

Juncos are easy to lure to a feeding station. Simply scatter cracked corn, millet and oil sunflower seeds directly on the ground – these ground birds shy away from tall feeders.

DISTRIBUTION AND IDENTIFICATION

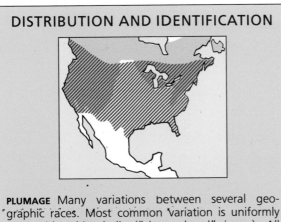

PLUMAGE Many variations between several geographic races. Most common variation is uniformly gray with white belly ("slate-colored" junco). All varieties show flash of white outer tail feathers in flight.

HABITAT Widespread in forested land.

FOOD Insects, seeds and berries; will eat cracked corn, millet, oil sunflower seed.

NEST Grass, moss and twigs, built on ground beneath overhanging vegetation or upturned tree roots.

EGGS 4–5 eggs; bluish with heavy brown speckling; wreathed.

WHITE-THROATED SPARROW
ZONOTRICHIA ALBICOLLIS

Like the junco, the white-throated sparrow is usually thought of as a winter visitor, a bird that breeds in the wild north country but retreats south in the face of the oncoming cold.

An adult white-throat is a dapper bird – gray breast, signature white throat, brown wings, and a boldly striped, white-and-black crown. Just in front of each eye is a tiny spot of yellow – the perfect touch.

In summer, the white-throat ranges from the Northwest Territories across central Canada to the Maritime Provinces and New England. It also occurs south into Pennsylvania, but only at high elevations. It is found most often in coniferous forests of spruce, fir or pine, with brushy undergrowth; in some areas they are associated with boggy locations, or mixed hardwoods and conifers.

Oh sweet Canada Canada Canada is the white-throat's musical, slightly quavery song, starting low, rising on the second note and dropping to a steady pitch for the rest.

In winter, white-throated sparrows flock together and migrate south, spreading out from the Northeast, across the South and into the Southwest; a small population also winters in southern California. The flocks stay in thickets, and show a fondness for swampy woods and dense stream banks, where poison ivy and other berry-producing plants have run riot. As spring approaches and the days grow longer, the birds begin to sing – hesitantly at first, then with growing conviction as the time for their return to the breeding grounds draws closer.

DISTRIBUTION AND IDENTIFICATION

PLUMAGE Gray breast, white throat, brown wings and boldly striped, white-and-black crown. Spot of yellow in front of each eye.

HABITAT Coniferous forests of spruce, fir or pine, with brushy undergrowth; also boggy locations.

FOOD Weed seeds and insects; berries in winter.

NEST Cup of grass, twigs and bark, built on ground.

EGGS 4–5 buffy eggs, heavily speckled with brown, especially at larger end.

WESTERN MEADOWLARK
STURNELLA NEGLECTA

The balladeer of the grasslands, the western meadowlark is one of the sweetest singers of the open plains. Drive down a prairie road on a spring morning, and its musical song floats through the open windows from the bird's fencepost perch.

Meadowlarks – both the western and the almost indistinguishable eastern species – are members of the blackbird group, but their family ties haven't carried over into color. The western meadowlark has a pale buff back, intricately streaked and spotted. Broad, dusky stripes mark the head, but the bird's most beautiful feature is its bright yellow throat and breast, with a black V hanging across it like a necklace. In flight, the meadowlark has a fat, short-tailed appearance, flashing white tail feathers that make an excellent field mark. Also distinctive is its habit of flying with its wings held below the horizontal, alternating long glides with periods of flapping.

The western meadowlark lives over a wide swath of North America, from southern Ontario to British Columbia, down into Mexico and east to Arkansas. It has been probing farther and farther to the northeast in recent years, overlapping the range of the eastern meadowlark. In the field it is almost impossible to separate the two species by sight (the western has slightly more yellow on the face), but, fortunately, the songs are completely different. The western's is a rich series of flute-like phrases, while the eastern's is short, sounding like *Spring of the ye-e-a-r.*

Grasshoppers, crickets, beetles and caterpillars make up the bulk of the western meadowlark's diet – bugs caught by hunting on the ground, among the clumps of prairie grass, with which the meadowlark's streaky pattern blends perfectly. The meadowlark is a ground nester, scraping a small hollow and then lining it with grasses, eventually building an arching roof to conceal the eggs from above. Where both occur, the western tends to pick drier areas to nest than the eastern, even though the two may live in the same pasture.

DISTRIBUTION AND IDENTIFICATION

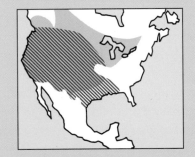

PLUMAGE Pale buff back, intricately streaked and spotted. Broad, dusky stripes on head; bright yellow throat and breast, with a black V "necklace". In flight, shows flashing white tail feathers.

HABITAT Grasslands and prairies.

FOOD Grasshoppers, crickets, beetles and caterpillars.

NEST Ground nest; a small hollow scraped and lined with grasses; with an arching roof.

EGGS 3–5 glossy white eggs with brown splotches.

RED-WINGED BLACKBIRD
AGELAIUS PHOENICEUS

raucaus *Ok-a-Le-e-e-e-e-e* calls, scarlet epaulets flashing in the sun. Fights are constant, as males jockey for the best locations, but by the time the females arrive about two weeks later, the boundaries are fairly well set.

Female red-wings are less visible than their mates, both behaviorally and in pattern. They are no less handsome, however – brown upperparts contrast with fine, dark steaking over a buff breast and head, with a light eyebrow stripe and a tinge of pink on the face. It is the female's job to build the nest, usually woven of sedges, reeds and grass over the water, among the upright stems of cattails. Where the habitat is good, red-wings nest in dense concentrations.

In the past 25 years, red-wings have greatly increased their numbers, in part because they have adapted to new nesting territories. No longer tied to wetlands, they now nest in pastures, alfalfa fields – anywhere with thick cover in which to hide their nests.

In winter they retreat south a bit, sometimes gathering in stunning numbers; bird-watchers in Little Rock, Arkansas, tallied an astonishing 13.4 million red-wings on the 1986 Audubon Christmas Bird Count there.

Ubiquitous in wetlands, pastures and hay fields across North America, the red-winged blackbird is so boisterous and distinctly marked that it is recognized by almost everyone.

Its range is all-encompassing: southern Alaska to Mexico, Newfoundland to Florida, and all points in between. And not only is the red-wing widespread, but it is abundant almost everywhere – one of the five most abundant species in North America, in fact.

The appearance of a male red-wing needs little introduction: glossy black plumage, with fiery red shoulder epaulets, rimmed at the bottom with a thin band of yellow.

Red-wings transform a spring marsh. What one day is a barren expanse of weathered, broken cattail spikes and rotting ice, the next becomes a circus of motion, color and sound when the red-wings return. The males come first, staking out their claims with

DISTRIBUTION AND IDENTIFICATION

PLUMAGE Male: glossy black, with fiery red shoulder epaulets, rimmed at bottom with yellow band. Female: brown upper parts, with fine dark streaking over buff breast and head, and a light eyebrow stripe and tinge of pink on face.

HABITAT Wetlands, pastures and hayfields.

FOOD Weed seeds, insects.

NEST Woven of sedges, leaves and grass over water, among stems of cattails.

EGGS 3–4 eggs; pale blue with brown scrawls.

BREWER'S BLACKBIRD
EUPHAGUS CYANOCEPHALUS

DISTRIBUTION AND IDENTIFICATION

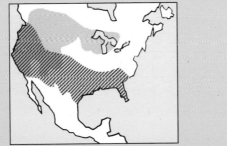

PLUMAGE Male: all-black, with shiny purple gloss to head. Female: dull brown overall.

HABITAT Open land, along roads and in fields.

FOOD Insects, seeds.

NEST Grass and mud cup; placement highly variable, from ground to high in trees.

EGGS 4–6 eggs; blue-gray with heavy brown splotches.

In much of the West, Brewer's blackbird is the most common, all-black bird – a widespread inhabitant of open land, often seen in large flocks along roads and in fields.

Slightly larger than a red-wing, the male Brewer's has a shiny, purple gloss to its head, and a pale, yellowish eye; the female is dull brown overall, with a dark eye. In the eastern half of its range, the Brewer's can easily be confused with the common grackle, a larger bird with a much longer tail and bill.

Like the western meadowlark (to which it is related), Brewer's blackbird has been pushing east, into the upper Midwest and Great Lakes region, since the turn of the century. The bulk of its summer range lies to the west, however, from the Canadian prairies to California, the mountain regions and parts of the Southwest. In winter, it migrates from the northern parts of its range, moving into much of the South.

During the breeding season, both male and female have ritualized displays that they use to attract mates, scare off rivals and cement the pair bond. One display, used as both a threat to intruding males and a preliminary to mating, is done by the male, who fluffs out his head and neck feathers while giving a squeaky call. In another threat posture, males will point their beaks skyward, stretching as tall as they can get.

Where the numbers of males and females are roughly equal, Brewer's blackbirds are usually monogamous, but if the ratio is skewed in favor of females, each male may have up to four mates. Such flexibility in pairing is found in other blackbirds as well, notably red-wings. While preferring open, tree-studded meadows for nesting, Brewer's blackbird is not fussy, and the nest may be anywhere from ground level to the branches of a tall tree.

COMMON GRACKLE
QUISCALUS QUISCULA

The smallest and most abundant of North America's three grackles, the common grackle is nevertheless a sizable songbird, reaching lengths of more than a foot – and appearing to be even bigger in flight, when it spreads its peculiarly keeled tail.

Grackles walk with an arrogant-seeming strut, head high, bright yellow eyes not missing a thing. This is a common suburban bird, quite at home with people; they are abundant in many city parks, and can be enticed to backyards fairly easily. Males are the glossiest, and come in two phases – one with a purple sheen, and the other with a bronze iridescence to its feathers. Females are duller, and young grackles are sooty brown, with a dark eye. The tail is rather long, and is usually held so that, when viewed from the rear, it forms a V.

The common grackle is found in summer in southern and central Canada, the Great Plains and Northeast, and year-round from the Midwest and Atlantic seaboard south to the Gulf Coast. They are insect, fruit and berry eaters, but are opportunists that will take whatever nature throws their way – freshly planted grain, frogs and toads, crayfish, minnows, the eggs and chicks of smaller birds, even mice, which they kill with blows of their heavy beaks.

A songbird by relation, not talent, the common grackle can do no better than a short, creaky song and a few harsh call notes.

Two other, larger grackle species have more restricted ranges. The boat-tailed grackle is found along the Mid-Atlantic and Gulf coasts, and the crow-sized, great-tailed grackle is a familiar town bird of the Southwest and Texas.

DISTRIBUTION AND IDENTIFICATION

PLUMAGE Male has 2 phases: one with purple sheen, other bronze iridescence to feathers; female duller. Long tail forms V from back.
HABITAT Most open areas – farmland, city parks and backyards.
FOOD Insects, fruits and berries mostly, but also grain, frogs, eggs, mice.
NEST Large mass of twigs, grass and weed stems in shrubs and trees; often nests in colonies.
EGGS 5–6 eggs; pale greenish with dark brown scrawls and splotches.

NORTHERN ORIOLE

ICTERUS GALBULA

A howl of protest went up from bird-watchers in the 1970s, when the American Ornithologists Union decided that the Baltimore oriole of the East, and the Bullock's oriole of the West, were only different races of the same species. Lumped together as the northern oriole, the two birds, quite different in plumage, are now treated as one because they hybridize in the Great Plains.

By whatever name, the northern oriole is a gorgeous bird. A male of the eastern race sports a black head and back, black wings with white wingbars, and a gloriously bright orange breast and belly. The female's pattern echoes the male's, but where he is orange, she is greenish. In the "Bullock's" race of the West, the male's pattern differs in having orange cheeks and black eyeline, and large white shoulder patches.

Ecologically and behaviorally, the two races are similar. Both like high deciduous trees, and "Baltimore" orioles have a special fondness for big walnuts, elms, hickories and oaks, growing in yards and other fairly open areas; they are also found at the forest edge, and along rivers and streams. "Bullock's" orioles stick to open woodlands, riverside cottonwoods and farmyards.

Even those with little interest in birds recognize an oriole's pendulous nest, one of the most remarkable in North America. The female starts by weaving long grasses around a high, forked tree branch (frequently one that overhangs water or a road). Working quickly, she forms the circular rim of the nest, then

DISTRIBUTION AND IDENTIFICATION

PLUMAGE Eastern-race male: black head and back, black wings with white wingbars and bright orange breast and belly. Western male: orange cheeks and black eyeline; large white shoulder patches.
HABITAT Both races favor high deciduous trees. Eastern race found in yards and open areas; also forest edges and by rivers and streams. Western race in open woodlands, riverside cottonwoods and farmyards.
FOOD Plant nectar, fruits.
NEST Pendulous, sturdy round bag, with long grasses woven around high, forked tree branch; circular rim has interlaced plant fibers, bark strips, yarn, etc.
EGGS 4–5 eggs; off white with dark scrawls and streaks.

spends the next several days interlacing plant fibers, bark strips, scavenged yarn and other stringy materials to build the hanging basket. The result is a sturdy, rounded bag to hold her four or five splotched eggs.

Many people have had success in luring orioles to the feeder by offering halved oranges. They also enjoy plant nectar, so special oriole feeders – large versions of hummingbird feeders – are available to cater to their taste.

WESTERN TANAGER
PIRANGA LUDOVICIANA

DISTRIBUTION AND IDENTIFICATION

PLUMAGE Male: bright yellow with black back and wings, yellow and white wingbars and bright orange-red head. Female: yellowish green, with faint wingbars. In winter male molts to resemble female, but with more prominent wingbars and red around the bill.
HABITAT Coniferous forests and mountains.
FOOD Wasps, bees, beetles, ants, caterpillars, fruits and berries.
NEST Shallow cup built of twigs, branches, conifer needles, moss and animal hair in the crotch of a pine branch high above ground.
EGGS 4–5 blue-green eggs with fine, brown spotting.

In the light-dappled gloom of a lodgepole pine forest, a sunbeam seems to take wing – a male western tanager, yellow and orange against the muted greens of the trees.

Common in coniferous forests and mountains over most of the West, from the Northwest Territories south to New Mexico and Arizona, the western tanager is an arresting sight, even for those who see the bird regularly. Just over seven inches long, the male is bright yellow, with a black back and wings, yellow and white wingbars and a bright orange-red head. The female, on the other hand, is plainly dressed in yellowish green, with faint wingbars.

Western tanagers eat large quantities of wasps and bees, as well as beetles, ants, caterpillars, fruits and berries.

Feeders stocked with orange slices may lure this gem of a songbird out of the trees and close to the house.

The nest is built in the crotch of a pine branch high above the ground, a shallow cup supporting four or five blue, speckled eggs, constructed of twigs, grasses, conifer needles, moss and animal hair. The breeding territory can be located by listening for the robin-like song of the male, who plays no part in nest-building, but will pitch in when the young hatch and need to be fed.

In winter, the western tanager migrates south into Mexico and Central America. By the time the southward journey begins, the male will have molted his flashy summer colors, taking on a plumage similar to the female's, but with more prominent wingbars and a bit of red around the bill.

SCARLET TANAGER
PIRANGA OLIVACEA

DISTRIBUTION AND IDENTIFICATION

PLUMAGE Male: vibrant red, with jet-black wings and tail. Female: solid yellow-green, slightly darker on back. Male molts after breeding, turning yellow-green like female, but retaining black wings; (during migration they are covered with blotches of red and green).
HABITAT High in the forest canopy of deciduous woodlands.
FOOD Insects.
NEST Small flimsy cup of rootlets, twigs, grass and weed stems, built far up in trees, up to 80-90 ft.
EGGS 4–5 eggs; faded blue-green with fine brown speckling.

Impossibly red, the male scarlet tanager looks like an exotic jungle inhabitant, instead of a common resident of northeastern forests. Actually, the bird's tropical appearance isn't as misleading as one might think, because the tanagers are primarily Central and South American birds, with only a few representatives that have colonized North America.

Whatever its heritage, a scarlet tanager is a stunning bird. The vibrancy of the red must be seen to be believed, and is accented further by the male's jet-black wings and tail. Yet despite his electric livery, the tanager is not seen without an effort, for it lives high in the forest canopy, where shifting sunlight and screening leaves hide it from human eyes.

Deciduous woodlands are home to the tanager, from the eastern Dakotas and Arkansas to the Carolinas and up into northern New England. The female is the same size as the male – seven inches – but is solid yellow-green, only slightly darker on the back.

The tanager spends virtually its entire summer in the highest reaches of the trees, especially oaks, patiently searching for insects in a slow, deliberate manner, with none of the frazzled energy that the smaller warblers exhibit. It will be from a distant treetop that the male's song will be heard, a lazy, hoarse series of notes. Beginning birders usually have trouble telling the difference between the songs of the tanager, robin, red-eyed vireo and rose-breasted grosbeak, for all have basically the same tone and rhythm. Recordings of bird songs, often marketed along with field guides, can help clear up the confusion.

The nest, typically, is built far up in the trees, at least 15 feet up and often as much as 80 or 90 feet high. The cup is small, built of rootlets, twigs, grass and weed stems, and is sometimes so flimsy that the eggs can be seen from below.

Like the western tanager, the male scarlet goes through a post-breeding molt, turning yellow-green like his mate, but with black wings. During the fall migration, many are seen mid-way through the process, covered with blotches of green and red.

HOUSE SPARROW
PASSER DOMESTICUS

In cities and backyards, farm feedlots and suburban parks, the house (or English) sparrow is everywhere. But like the house mouse and Norway rat, this European immigrant survives only in association with people, and can rarely tolerate a truly wild situation.

While the origin of the European starling can be traced to a single introduction, the house sparrow had many sponsors. As early as 1850, it was being released in the hope that it would control cankerworm, a major pest of trees. By the end of the 1800s, this little bird was found all across the continent, often in tremendous numbers. It quickly made a mark, also, on other birds, usurping the nest cavities of many native species, particularly bluebirds and purple martins.

The house sparrow's numbers have dropped somewhat since the turn of the century, in part, some authorities believe, because the car has replaced the horse, eliminating a year-round supply of seeds in the manure. In parts of the Northeast, newly introduced house finches from the American West are replacing house sparrows almost completely.

It hardly seems necessary to offer a description of the house sparrow; it is so abundant that almost everyone is familiar with it. The male's black bib and chestnut nape are unmistakable, as are the female's gray breast and buffy eye-stripe. In winter the male's black bib is reduced to a small throat patch, or so it

DISTRIBUTION AND IDENTIFICATION

PLUMAGE Male: black bib and chestnut nape. Female: gray breast and buffy eye-stripe.

HABITAT Backyards, cities, parks, etc.; rarely in the wild.

FOOD Seeds, manure.

NEST Collection of grass, leaves, feathers, trash, stuffed into any available cranny, from chimneys to drainpipes.

EGGS 5–7 greenish-white eggs with brown spots.

appears. Actually, the newly molted bib feathers have buffy tips, which will wear away by spring, revealing the black beneath – a process called feather erosion.

The house sparrow's nest is a collection of grass, weeds, leaves, feathers and trash, stuffed into any available cranny. The list of acceptable nest sites includes everything from chimneys and porch eaves to birdboxes, drainpipes and stoplight covers.

AMERICAN GOLDFINCH
CARDUELIS TRISTIS

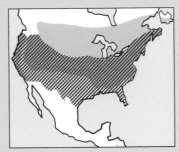

PLUMAGE Male: bright yellow, with black cap set low over beak; black wings with white wingbars and black tail. Female: subtle olive, with touches of yellow at throat. In winter male molts into a buffy olive.
HABITAT Pastures and fields.
FOOD Small seeds of thistles; oil sunflower seed and African niger, or "thistle" seed, at feeder.
NEST Built inside rising branches of shrub or sapling with a multiple fork; outer shell of weed leaves and grass, most of soft, gray thistledown.
EGGS 4–5 pale bluish-white eggs.

In the rich farmland of south-central Pennsylvania, the farmers of German descent called it the "dusselfink," the thistle finch – a fitting name for the American goldfinch, which has shifted its breeding cycle to coincide with the ripening of thistles in late summer.

Many more people know this small bird as the "wild canary," named for the male's bright yellow color. It is well-loved, as much a tribute to its ease around people as its plumage.

Only about five inches long, the goldfinch has a round head and a short tail. The male is lemon yellow, with a black cap set low over the beak, black wings with white wingbars, and a black tail. The female is a more subtle shade of olive, with touches of yellow at the throat. The call, often given in flight, is a brisk *per-chickory, per-chickory.*

The American goldfinch occurs in a wide band across North America in summer, avoiding only the far north, southern coastal plain and Southwest. In winter it pulls out of the northern edge of its range as far south as the Gulf Coast, but toughs out the bad weather as far north as Maine. It is a common winter feeder bird, although at that time of year the males have molted into a buffy olive plumage very much like the female's. Oil sunflower seeds and "thistle" seeds (actually African niger) are eaten most often.

In July and August, the big bull thistles are ripening in pastures and fields across the continent. Cursed by ranchers and farmers, thistles are the staff of life to goldfinches, which feed on the small seeds and use the fluffy thistledown to build their nests. A small shrub or sapling with a multiple fork is chosen, and the nest is built inside the rising branches, which support it like exterior columns. The outer shell is made of weed leaves and grass, but most of the nest is soft, gray thistledown, into which the half-dozen white eggs are laid.

HOUSE FINCH
CARPODACUS MEXICANUS

A native of the West, the house finch has become an eastern city-slicker, following its introduction in New York in 1940 – according to one story, by pet dealers who didn't want to be nabbed with a shipment of these protected songbirds.

Since then its numbers have exploded, and so has its range, as the species leap-frogs each year into new territory. It now occupies most of the continent east of the Mississippi, mystifying those using older field guides that don't show it occurring anywhere near their area.

The house finch is a sparrow-sized bird with a small, conical bill. The male is brown, with a cardinal-red breast, rump and face. The females are covered with smudgy, brown streaking, and can appear plain brown in some plumages.

In the West, the house finch is most common in agricultural lands and residential areas, although it is less wedded to man than those in the East, and can be found in canyons, wooded hillsides and even rather far up into the mountains. The nest is neat and tidily made, placed in small trees, bushes or birdboxes. In the East, house finches have shown an inordinate attraction to hanging baskets of houseplants and flowers, frequently excavating a small depression in the potting soil that is then lined with grass and plant fibers. In some areas, a pair may raise two or three

DISTRIBUTION AND IDENTIFICATION

PLUMAGE Male: brown, with cardinal-red breast, rump and face. Female: covered with smudgy brown streaking.
HABITAT Common in agricultural lands and residential areas, as well as canyons and even mountains.
FOOD Insects, seeds and berries; common feeder.
NEST Neatly made and placed in small trees, bushes or birdboxes; in East attracted to hanging baskets of houseplants, excavating a small depression in the potting soil then lined with grass and plant fibers.
EGGS 4–6 pale blue-green eggs with fine brown speckling.

broods of young, with up to a half-dozen chicks per brood – one reason why its numbers are growing so rapidly.

House finches are easy to bring to a feeder – sometimes too easy. Winter flocks may total more than 100 birds, and can quickly take over the situation.

EVENING GROSBEAK
COCCOTHRAUSTES VESPERTINUS

Big and beautiful, evening grosbeaks are favorites at the bird feeder, but they are also terribly fickle migrants, invading much of the U.S. in some years, all but absent in others.

Birds of the Canadian forest and western mountains, they are eight inches long and heavyset, equipped with thick, seed-crushing bills. Males are yellow on the underside and back, with brown heads, yellow eyebrows and black wings that show large areas of white. The females are equally attractive, with muted shades of gray, buff and yellow.

In the coniferous forests where they breed, evening grosbeaks generally nest at least 15 feet above the ground, and often much higher than that. The twig, moss and lichen nest is built by the female. The chicks are fed a steady diet of insects, especially spruce budworm, but later switch to the adults' fare of seeds, berries and fruit, augmented by insects.

The evening grosbeak's seasonal movements are too erratic to be called a migration, and might best be termed wandering. Unlike most birds, grosbeaks generally move in a northwest-to-southeast direction, rather than due south. In years when the cone crop in the spruce and pine forests is good, most may stay on their breeding grounds. But if the crop is lean (about every two or three years), they fan out over a wide area, sometimes going as far southeast as the Gulf Coast.

Interestingly, evening grosbeaks were unknown east of the Mississippi prior to about 1890, and almost every year they nudge the limits of their winter range a little farther south. It is speculated that box elders, widely planted across the formerly treeless prairies, provided a new supply of seeds that lured the wintering flocks east.

At the feeder, evening grosbeaks like sunflower seeds – and lots of them. A flock can go through incredible quantities in a short time, earning this species the half-joking nickname "gross-pigs."

DISTRIBUTION AND IDENTIFICATION

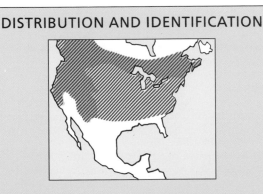

PLUMAGE Male: yellow on underside and back, with brown head, yellow eyebrows and black wings with large areas of white. Female: muted shades of gray, buff and yellow; black wings with white areas.
HABITAT Coniferous forests; move into parks and backyards in winter if natural crop lean.
FOOD Insects, seeds, berries and fruit; love sunflower seeds at feeder.
NEST Twig, moss and lichen, at least 15 ft above ground.
EGGS 3–4 blue eggs with brown blotches.

INDEX

ACKNOWLEDGMENTS AND PICTURE CREDITS

The author and publishers would like to thank Doug Wechsler at VIREO for organizing the provision of photographs. Map artwork is by Ellie King.

C R Sams II and J F Stoick; pp 2, 34, 42, 50, 59, 73r, 911; B Schorre: pp 6, 62, 63, 64, 70, 71, 74, 76, 89; G Dremeaux: pp 7, 33, 40; R & M Hansen: pp 8, 80, 87, 93; J R Woodward: pp 9, 18r, 20, 25, 27, 31, 35r, 37, 39, 46r, 48, 51, 52, 73l, 82; H Cruickshank; pp 10, 11, 19, 38, 83, 86, 88; A Morris: pp 12, 21, 45, 56; F K Schleicher: p 14; C Mohr: pp 15, 551; J Dunning: p 16; D Weschler: pp 17, 85; W Greene; pp 18l, 23l, 26, 46l, 57, 67, 75; D & M Zimmerman: pp 22, 61, 72; C H Greenewalt: pp 23r, 24, 35l, 43, 53, 58, 60, 68; J D Young: pp 28, 65l; H Clarke: pp 29, 32, 49, 65r, 66, 92; S Holt: p 30; F Lanting: p 36; B Randall: pp 41, 44, 47, 54; O S Pettingill: p 55r; S J Lang: pp 69, 77, 81, 84; T Fitzharris: p 78; P La Tourette: p 79; R Villani: p 90; R Schallenberger: p 91r.